MW01170948

FOUND IN MY WORLD

Terrance McAdoo

McAdoo Publishing Company

Copyright © 2024 by Terrance McAdoo All rights reserved.

ISBN: 979-8-9901855-0-0 (digital)

ISBN: 979-8-9901855-1-7 (paperback)

ISBN: 979-8-9901855-2-4 (hardback)

No part of this book may be reproduced, distributed, or transmitted in any form or by any means, including, but not limited to: photocopying, recording, scanning, or by any information storage and retrieval system, or other electronic or mechanical methods without the prior written permission from the author.

Printed in the United States of America

Table of Contents

1.	Homeless	1
2.	A Trip to Remember	10
3.	Unusual Times	24
4.	College Graduation	37
5.	Crack Is A POWERFUL Drug!	45
6.	Throwing in the Tile	53
7.	Missing Piece to My Puzzle	58
8.	Dead End	65
9.	Need Relaxation.	76
10.	Mixed Emotions	82
11.	Life of Curve Balls	92
12.	Back on Track	110
13.	Slow Down! Slow Down!	119
14.	Welcome to Atlantis!	132
15.	A New Horizon	151
16.	Life Amongst the Whites	162
17.	What Do Elephants Eat? Deez Nutz	184
18.	Downgrade	198
19.	Bottom Line	209

PROLOGUE

Learning that my mother has breast cancer is only the beginning of my life crashing in front of my eyes. She had beat cancer before, but it had reappeared years later. I am the youngest out of three siblings. I then meet Ladonna, who looks identical to my ex-girlfriend, Brenda, who was murdered during the summer of my junior year in high school. Though family members and friends tried to warn me that I was making a terrible mistake being in a relationship with her, I didn't listen.

Though Ladonna frequently breaks up with me, over little arguments, I never gave up hope. I felt as if Brenda's reincarnated, and no matter what, I wasn't going to lose her a second time; especially since she became my first love.

Time and time again I put all my faith and effort into our relationship which inevitably blows up. And now, we have a child on the way, and I just lost my job and depression is setting in. As I'm filling out numerous job applications, I contemplate a catastrophic event and then act upon it. I break into a trailer at my previous job, where they keep clothes to distribute to different stores, and empty a 5-gallon gas tank inside. But I'm so angry over my wrongful termination that I didn't notice the gas splashing on me. I grab my lighter and *whoosh!* my clothes erupt in flames, as well as everything else in the trailer. I barely crawl out in time, and though I am badly burned, I'm alive.

Now that my mom passed from breast cancer, the only option is to move in with my sister, Keisha, and pay rent. I lean on her for emotional support about being in love, but she would always give advice that I didn't want to hear, leaving me feeling more confused than ever.

With a newborn child, it's time that I kick it into high gear by choosing a career and getting a job that has tuition reimbursement to help pay for my college. After I let my wounds heal, I went out on a search. I ended up at E-Box, a package shipping company, while still going to college to be an electrician. I use my morning and lunch breaks to catch up on much needed sleep.

Time goes on and the relationship between Ladonna and I become violent. Then her dad, Mr. Walker, put a knife to my stomach. Though no one was hurt, all three of us went to jail, putting my college education and job on the line. The case gets dismissed, and just like all the other times, we ignore the past and make up. Our family members can't understand why we were putting ourselves and our child through a dysfunctional relationship. But Ladonna_and I were holding onto an agreement we made when she first became pregnant: no matter what, we won't let our son grow up with single parents.

Despite all the drama, I still managed to graduate from Technical College in the electrical field. My ambition is compared to those of the extraordinary. Now I only have to wait until graduation day, but I push fate to the limit again resulting in the police being called, which causes me to lose my job at E-Box. When I no longer can make rent, I was kicked out. My brother makes fun of me for it and we get in a brawl outside. Now, the only option left for me is to pack my bags and enter the dark and loneliest stage of my life: being homeless and sleeping inside my vehicle.

CHAPTER 1
HOMELESS

What the fuck? What will happen now? Am I really gonna do this? How long will I be living like this? I cannot believe what is going on. I'm homeless now. Should I just go back and try to apologize to my sister, Keisha, for trying to work things out with Ladonna, the mother of my child, and her putting me through all of this? Naw. She locked the door. She locked me out of her life. Besides, I can't just blame Ladonna. I also play a part in it.

Those were the emotions tumbling through my head at that very moment. Ladonna and I had been playing Russian roulette with our toxic relationship. *Click. Click. Click. Bang!* In the end, the bullet had fired upon *me* pulling the trigger.

Ladonna could still live comfortably in her apartment, while I had to shelter myself in my blue Ford Explorer. On the bright side, it was an SUV, so I had more room to work with than in a normal size car. Whatever came my way, I knew I had to deal with it and just know the Lord would be with me every step of my journey… if I truly had faith like I claimed. My mother's words came back to me, "Just keep going." I didn't start up my truck and leave right away. I had to take in the present moment. What it looked like, what objects were around me. I was shocked. I never thought I would become homeless. Sure, I'd heard of people becoming homeless because of alcohol issues, drug addiction, gambling addiction, or just giving up on life, but not this.

It felt as if time was standing still. The only thing that was moving at that time of the night were gnats flying around the streetlights. As I was about to start up my truck to leave, I looked around and saw it was filled with all my stuff. Thankfully, I'd packed a cover and pillow. It was late September and temperatures would start to plummet in late October. The brutal winter season was staring me dead in the eyes. I knew I had to be prepared. There was no room to fit anything else in my truck. That withdrew the energy from me that I needed to escape, seeing all of this was real. I sat around for another ten minutes. "The longer I sit here, the harder it will be to leave," I said to myself. And I knew going back and talking to Keisha about staying was not an option. I started up my truck, thinking I would drive until my mind became clearer on what to do next.

As I was driving around, I knew I had one option to survive. Labor Forcer temp agency. The most I ever made in a week there was right under $100. It wasn't enough to get me out of my vehicle and into a motel room for the week, but it would keep gas in my tank and food in my stomach.

I remembered a spot where I could park. It was a small, grassy field church parking lot close to where I once lived when I was younger. That would be my campsite for the duration of my homelessness, so I thought. But destiny had another route for me. A cop wound up responding to a complaint and telling me I could no longer stay there, but I'll save that for later in the story. Other than Sundays, rarely did anyone ever park there. That space was only used if all the parking spaces close to the church were filled up. I figure I could be there as long as I needed without being bothered.

I still had tension in my mind from that fight I'd had with my relative, Druski. I knew if I did something stupid like the arson that I pulled because I was fired from Goodpo. The odds of me being satisfied after the situation were slim to none. Going forward after that situation I'd think twice when I wanted to react to something just to get revenge. Being trapped in a burning trailer with walls of fire surrounding you and not seeing a way out will make you think twice about committing a crime like that ever again.

My clothes were still damp from Druski and I tussling around on the wet grass. Me sleeping? Nope. I knew I couldn't even take a cat nap, no matter how many sleeping aids I took. It was six hours until I had to get up and go to Labor Forcer and hope my name would get called to go out for work. I moved everything I had from my passenger seat and stuffed it in the back. I needed more legroom, and that was the best spot at the time. I reclined the seat all the way back and tried to get comfortable. Being homeless didn't scare me, it just filled my mind with curiosity. It was wondering around like crazy. I was twenty-two years old when all of this happened, which is too young to be put in this type of situation. I thought, *what am I going to do with my life now*? One thing was for certain, I wasn't going to let it all run me crazy and cause me to lose my only dependable shelter and live under a bridge or stay at a homeless shelter. After my mind replayed back the events which put me where I was— seemed like a love-drama movie—it was time for me to head to Labor Forcer.

I had parked in a way so people couldn't see inside my car. And if they somehow did ask about the pile of bags and other miscellaneous items, my excuse would be that I was moving. I was emotionally and physically drained. I had no fight left in me. My body was now shut down from society. It was hard for me to even smile. It took a great deal for me not to drop my head, slouch my shoulders, and drag my feet. I tried to keep a low profile. I didn't want anyone to know about my current situation. It would be embarrassing for me to tell someone I was homeless. I knew that if I told even *one person*, it would quickly spread like wildfire. That would be the breaking point of me not ever returning to that place again. Then I would really be at my lowest point. As I calmly walked to the desk to sign the attendance sheet at Labor Forcer, I was stopped,

"Are you okay?" a co-worker asked.

"Yeah, I'm good."

She continued to walk on to find a seat. The receptionist asked me the same question after I signed in.

"You don't seem like yourself today… if it's Jake, I will beat him up for you."

Jake was just another co-worker waiting to be called out for work like me.

With a blank look I answered, "Naw he cool."

Why is everybody asking if I'm okay? I thought to myself. My pants looked half decent, as they always had looked, and my shirt wasn't stretched out or ripped. Perhaps what they were seeing wasn't on my front, where I could see, maybe my shirt was ripped in the back or something. After thinking that might be what was up I went to the restroom to glance in the mirror. The guy looking back at me in that mirror had the meanest look on his face, like the entire world was against him. It felt comfortable though, so I guess that's why it stuck. What I'd just gone through hours ago was literally life changing. I gathered myself together and went back out to find a seat. I flopped down in a chair that was furthest away from everybody and waited *patiently,* hoping that my name got called out for work. What I'm about to say is sad to say - money was my main priority at that point. My son was not. He was too young to understand his parents' circumstances anyway.

I was hoping to be called out on a job that required minimal communication, and preferably a job working alone. My mouth was glued shut from depression. Conversation didn't exist anymore. That moment was like a blur.

Later on that day, after work, I drove around and got a little bite to eat. I still had some cash on me to make it through the week. There was no need to waste my gas. I parked at my sleeping spot and walked to the basketball court of an elementary school. There was nothing else to do, and friends were not around. I didn't trust any of them enough to share such sensitive information anyway. After I played ball by myself, I went walking around my old neighborhood and reminisced about the good ole days. It was getting dark, and it was time for me to be stuck in my vehicle. I fell asleep for a little while, but due to the new environment my body couldn't get comfortable enough to stay asleep. For the remainder of the night, I fought hard trying to go back to sleep, but my mind wouldn't settle down. I stayed up, tossing and turning, until it was time for me to head off to work the next day.

As I went into the building, I tried to have a positive mindset so I wouldn't have an angry look on my face like the previous day. I even told a couple of people good morning. That must have took too much energy because, after that, I didn't want anyone to even make eye contact with me. That would signal me to engage in a conversation, which was a challenge to speak at all. My body was still in a *depressed* state.

Three days had passed, and no one had noticed the piled-up clothes in my vehicle. Dodged a big bullet there. I was starting to smell like hot garbage and needed some place to wash up and change clothes, so I stopped over at Ladonna's momma's house, Ms. Spank. Even though Ladonna and I weren't on good terms, she didn't hold that against me. I told her that my sister and I weren't getting along and so I had moved out into my uncle's place. Then I said that he was down on his luck. His water was shut off, and that was why I needed a place to take a shower. Everything I told her was a total made-up fairytale, but she believed me. Taking a nice, hot, steamy shower relieved some stress. She didn't have to pay no water bill, so

I took advantage of it and let my body soak till I looked like a prune. She was cool with me, so I hung out at her house with her and Ladonna's brother, Demetrius, until nighttime. Then it was back to the grass field I went. That couldn't be a regular thing though, because I knew she would soon catch on if I went over there every day until I could find a place on my own.

Arriving at my spot, I slid over into the passenger seat, kicked my feet up on the dash and began to think. As I was talking to myself, my mind began to come up with a strategic plan,

> "*I can go over there Mondays and Fridays, maybe a day in between, depending on how dirty I am from the job I was put on for that day. When I'm not over there, maybe I can chill here to save money. Playing ball every day will get boring. Leaving work, coming back here, and staying in my vehicle until it's time to go to sleep, then to work, and then doing it all over again is gonna be bad for me mentally. Why am I having a full-blown conversation with myself? Am I starting to get crazy in the head? Hahahaha.*"

I stared at all the things behind me, and noticed I needed to make some room.

> *"Where can I put all my stuff? Ms. Spank's house? Nope, she would ask why it isn't over at my uncle's house... and that would be a dead giveaway. I can't just leave it sitting out on the ground. A storage facility... yeah, and there's one up the street from where I'm at. I need to do that after work tomorrow. That's my plan."*

After I got off work, I followed through with my plan and got all the details I would need to store all my stuff in there. I didn't need a big one, so I'd just get the smallest unit with the lowest monthly payment. Everything worked out just the way I wanted it to. I had enough money to get it right then, but I would be dead broke. So I saved up more than enough money from work, and then rented out a unit. I took a sigh of relief after getting back inside my vehicle, "*ahhh, finally, some more room.*" I still had a couple of my items inside: covers, pillows, and a change of clothes. Everything was in a neat pile behind the back row seats. Now I can charge for carpool to make extra cash. It was a rule for workers who can't provide transportation for themselves to pay drivers $5 for gas. Work was coming in at a steady pace and the money started to pour in. The more workers I got to ride with me, the more money I made, which meant the better my circumstances would get.

There were sometimes when a worker would say he would pay me the next day, but never did. One time, I had five people with me. I knew I was going to make a good profit for that trip. They all worked at the same place, except me. I was waiting on a call for somewhere else. The next day, only two people paid me. The rest said they would pay me the following day. They didn't even show up the next day. In fact, that was the first and last time I ever saw them. I was burnt out of $15. I know that may not seem like a lot, but when you are homeless, every *penny* counts.

I was still going to do carpool though, but from then on out I planned to take whoever didn't pay to the nearest place after work where they cash checks and get my money right then. No excuses! I told the receptionist that I will no longer carry a large group of people to work unless I was on the job with them. She totally agreed, and from that point forward I never had any more issues with me receiving my gas money.

I was now starting to adapt to my homeless situation. When it was time for bed, I would let my back seats down to create space big enough for my long legs to be fully stretched out. I had one cover I slept on, and I put Mom's quilt over the top of me. Those days became weeks, and in the back of my mind I started to wonder how long I'd be living like this without anyone catching on, and how long it'd be before I found a place I could call home. It was stressful not knowing, but for the time being I would just have to go with the flow. I was trying to stretch every dollar. McDonalds was the ideal place for that. The dollar menu was my friend. The fries and a burger that I bought in the afternoon would satisfy my hunger until that evening. Before bed, there was another order of the same thing. For drinks, I'd ask for a water cup and fill it up with soda. Most of the time, the employees would give me a soda cup anyways. They must have been tired of catching people doing it, so they went on and gave you what you *didn't* ask for. After work, I found myself going to the projects to play basketball. There was always someone on the court, and it was better than playing by myself at the school. That was how I filled my days until it was bedtime. Then I'd wake up and do it all again, day in and day.

My coworkers quickly realized how much of a hard worker I was. It wasn't just because of me being homeless and wanting to shine so they'd keep me on jobs though, being a hard worker is in my blood. When work came in, the receptionist knew she could count on me to get the job done in an orderly fashion. Other people would take long breaks, perform sloppy work, or both. Seven days a week, Labor Forcer had work. I was there every day, even on Saturdays. Sundays were the only days you could be a sign holder. A sign holder? Yup. You know the people that you see on street corners flipping around signs advertising businesses like pizza spots, mattress stores, phone companies, and other establishments. But I'd only do that job if I *desperately* needed the money. At this point, I was doing okay.

My career as an electrician was put on hold due to the lack of work being bided out, but I made sure that if they needed any electrical work done, I was their guy. I had finished college with a diploma in electrical systems from a technical college. The next step was to wait on my big graduation day to walk across the stage. I didn't even know when that day was. I wasn't sure if I was going to attend or not. It was something very important to me. I put in the work and the time. The big finale was the pay off, when I'd walk across the stage with a big smile on my face and all my friends and family would witness my accomplishment. But that was it, no one would be there that really knew me, only my teachers and colleagues. My family didn't want nothing to do with me. If I had asked them to come out on my big day and they rejected my offer. That would crush me.

Ladonna? Nope, she was out of the question. *Friends?* What friends? Some were locked up or hustling on the streets. I had thought about hustling on the block, since it was quick money, but knew that I'd eventually get caught up in the hype and wind up sitting in jail. My vehicle would get taken from me if that happened. And since I had nobody to call to bail me out and didn't have enough money to bail myself out either, I would lose everything I had in storage and would have to build myself up again from the bottom. Even lower than I already was. As bad as that place might have seemed, I was at least going to work, I had a somewhat comfortable spot to sleep, and reliable transportation. I didn't have any more time to waste my life away. It was put up or shut up.

On one of my crazy hair days, I stopped over at Ms. Spank's house to see if she knew anyone that could braid. She asked around and found Tracy. She walked into Ms. Spank's living room and instantly I was frozen. I knew God could create such beautiful masterpieces, but this right here was the queen of all queens. He really took his time with her, like she was going to be the last female sculpture that He would ever create. Those light brown eyes of hers matched her brown skin. The body was bonus! *Thank you God for sending her to me. But damn... why she had to be so little?* She had to be no taller than 5'3 standing on her tippy toes. Maybe it was just the fact that I'm so tall—standing at 6'3, flat footed—that made her look so damn small. I don't know, but I do know that a real girl isn't perfect, and a perfect girl isn't real. At the time, I was twenty-two and she was twenty-nine.

She sat down slowly on the couch, and I sat down closely by her legs on the floor. She didn't want to stand and do it. "Watch the baby," Ms. Spank said. Distracted by Tracy's beauty, I barely heard her. We began to chit-chat about random things. She was the type of woman I was looking for. She believed in God and brought a lot to the table. She could cook and didn't smoke. The only "alcoholic" drink she loved was long island iced teas. She was a good mom to her kid, kept the house clean, and kept her kid disciplined. She had her own place, which meant she liked to be independent like me. I were thinking, *this will be my future boo*.

When I had gathered all the information on her love life, which she didn't have anymore, that girl was *mine.* I just had to pick the *perfect* time to ask her out. But first, I had to show her what kind of man she would have if she chose me. My situation of being homeless was temporary, so I didn't feel the need to spill the beans on that sensitive subject yet. If I had told her that during our conversation, that would have been the only thing she thought about whenever she saw me. Which would surely equal a confident *no* whenever I did ask her out.

"Watch my stomach," Tracy said.

"Huh, what, you talking to me?"

"Umm *yeahhh*."

"What's wrong with your stomach?" I asked, sounding confused.

It wasn't until I turned around that I was amazed.

"I'm pregnant."

I couldn't see her stomach at first, but while she was braiding my hair, she took off her jacket and boom! There was a nice size baby growing in her. She had to have been at least five months pregnant. Oh my! How am I going to handle this now? Being with someone that was pregnant, and with a baby that isn't mine was a whole different thing. It all made sense then... no wonder why she sat down so slowly like that, and that was what Ms. Spank was talking about when she said to watch the baby. I thought for a moment... yeah, I should keep pressing on. She is unique. I gave myself excuses so it wouldn't seem so bad being with a pregnant woman whose baby isn't mine. Maybe the baby's father chickened out, and now she's on her own. And doing quite well, I should add. She already had one and this baby would be number two. When she had finished braiding my hair, I asked her how much she charged.

"You can give me whatever."

In my mind I took this as a flirtatious response. Normally the people that do my hair know how much they are going to charge for their service, but this one was different.

Joking around I said, "How about $5?" I waited to hear her comment on my low wages.

"Yeah, that's cool."

I was still waiting on some sort of laughter, but there wasn't any.

"Naw, I can't do you like that. You're a single mother, here's $10."

I couldn't believe she went that low for doing such a good job on my head.

"Yeah, $10 would be good," she said.

She took my money and headed on her way. She was my new hairdresser. Nobody ever charged me that little to do my hair. It was always $15 or $25. I didn't get her number that day, because I knew she would be easy to find whenever I needed my hair done again. Plus, she lived up the street from Ms. Spank. I needed to grow some balls very, very soon and ask her out before somebody take this angel and mistreat her. *Again.*

CHAPTER 2
A TRIP TO REMEMBER

James, my uncle's son, now had ownership of my mom's house when she died, and my sister Michelle was living there at the time. There was still some of my mom's furniture left in the house. She was not having it when James decided to demand rent at the house we grew up in and stayed at most of our lives. She then began to save so that she could move out as quickly as possible.

When she did move out, that's when the locks were changed and the house that once belonged to us became one we could no longer enter. It had become abandoned until James could find a suitable renter for it. The house sat there for months, with no "For Rent" sign posted anywhere. Simply using my key to unlock the door and live *free* was out of the question. If there was any other way to get inside, I would figure it out. I thought about living in the basement. Looking through the window, I could see the old couch that folded out into a bed. There was no fireplace to keep me warm, but at least I would be sleeping somewhere I could *temporarily* call my home.

All the windows around the house were old. The latch was broken on the basement window. If I was going to get in, that would be the way. I moved the miscellaneous items that were packed outside in front of it. Mom didn't want anyone to know that particular window was easy to open. I felt paranoid to break into my *own* home for comfort. I was going back and forth, checking all around the house to make sure no one would see me as I would look like a burglar doing what I was about to. I never did feel comfortable about it, but I knew it was something that had to be done. I lifted the window, stuck my head in, and looked around. *Yup, this would be a good spot to lay my head at.* It felt good to be back at my old stomping grounds. Getting through the window was no problem. Once in, I started to set up my living quarters.

Getting upstairs from the basement was only prevented by a latch on the door. If I could get past that then I could enter the house. I took a sharp piece of thin metal I found laying on the ground and used that to remove the hook from the latch. I was in. But the power had been cut off. I took the old candles Mom had for decorations. Back then, even if we didn't have power, she wouldn't touch them. Mom kept separate candles for those times. In this case, she wasn't around to stop me. I was going to use them so I could see my way around when the natural sunlight faded away and left me in darkness.

Later that night, I had everything set up. I lit all the candles I had gathered from upstairs. I wasn't going to put them out until I became too tired from watching the flame flicker or talking to myself for entertainment. As I began to doze off, I noticed the candles were going out by themselves due to the wax buildup. One less thing I had to worry about. If I did fall asleep, the candles would put themselves out by the time I woke up. And the floor was concrete, so I wouldn't have to worry about it catching on fire if somehow the candles did fall to the ground. But then I started to wonder. In this huge basement, how would I see if it became pitch black and I wanted to go outside and couldn't find my lighter? So I got up and cleared a path straight to the garage door. Once I made it to the garage door, the only thing I had to do was lift it up to get out.

There was no reason for me to go anywhere at that time of night anyway, so I was good no matter what. Being alone in a gigantic basement made me feel uncomfortable and I couldn't get relaxed enough to fall asleep. I tried hard to tell myself everything was going to be okay.

"Nobody is here and if somebody does come, well… I will cross that bridge when I get there. This is only temporary, but I can't wait till I get my shit together. This is stupid, me living here. I don't even think I will be able to fall asleep tonight. If I can only hit the lottery, I'm gone and won't ever live like this again. Please God, help me get back on my feet."

I wanted to just keep my mind focused on the good times. Good Times? The only good time I can remember is when I was living with Mom. I'm in this old basement now. No one to talk to on the outside, and no company to keep my mind off things. Where will I go from here? Don't know. I will just have to keep living day by day and hope for the best. Just then, I noticed creaking sounds coming from inside the house. It was the wooden floors upstairs.

"That is just my imagination." I know your mind can trick you to make you see or hear something when it is nothing at all. I had one eye open and one eye closed, just in-case my imagination was right this time. A couple of minutes went by and there was no noise present. My body was so exhausted, I just wanted to go to sleep. *Creakkkkkkkkk.* There it was again. I didn't open my eyes that time. It became mind-boggling when I heard what sounded like someone upstairs, walking around. "What da hell is that?" I sat up on the sofa bed. My candles had a very low flame. I emptied out the wax to make the flame grow.

"I don't know if I can do this. There's something moving upsta—"

I was interrupted by the sound of footsteps. The sound would go in one direction, and then in the other. And the spot where I kept hearing it was in the hallway. I wasn't going to dare try to communicate with what I assumed were spirits. That house is where my mother took her last breath. I would've had a heart attack if I had asked,

"Who is there?" and it answered back,

"It's me. Your momma."

Once I heard the floors creaking again in the hallway, I was out of there. Nope! I was not about to stay in there! Back to my vehicle I went. I have gained enough wisdom by watching movies to know if it's not bothering me, then I won't bother it. I am Black, not stupid. Only a fool would go and see what is causing all the noise… *Splat!!!* That person is dead, and the remains are *unknown,* or they just become demonic. Nope! Not me. Black people run from paranormal activity, or shoot in that direction and then only after the clip is empty ask, "Are you still there?" I blew out the candles and got the hell out of the basement as quickly as I could.

Being homeless sucks! At least most homeless people hang out with each other. I was trying to keep a low profile though, because I was too embarrassed to share such sensitive information with anyone. My boredom took control of my mind in a negative way. I started to remember ways you can commit suicide without causing torment to yourself. I had a basement and a vehicle. When your car is running, it produces carbon monoxide. If you inhale enough of that toxic gas it makes the human body fall asleep peacefully. This is sad to say, but if I didn't get out of that situation soon, that would be my end resort. But first I had to check a very important thing—something I'd always wanted to do—off my bucket list.

All my life I wanted to attend The University of Michigan. Maize and Blue are the colors pumping through my veins. It was one of my top three things to do before I left this earth. I got all my stuff out of storage and used the basement. Now I can start saving again and hopefully have more than enough money to make it all the way to Michigan and take a personal tour around campus. Even if I didn't have enough, it was a trip I needed to experience by any means necessary.

In the meantime, I was playing the lottery every week and hoping that God would answer my prayers and let me win the jackpot. Then I wouldn't have to ever think about being homeless again. I started off just playing occasionally. Over time, I gradually became obsessive with it. I failed week after week, not even matching up one number to win a dollar. My next strategy was to buy enough tickets to defy the odds of winning, so I could be guaranteed to walk away with some kind of dollar amount. That was also a failure. To me, it seemed like the only way of making it out of my homeless situation. The other way was just to simply die.

Work was coming at such a steady pace that I was getting called out every day. The sun parted the clouds, and life was finally cutting me some slack. I saved up no more than $250 when I decided to go balls to the wall and take my trip. I got my directions from MapQuest website and printed them off (that was the old way to navigate your way around, before GPS).

Later on that night, I took off. It was an exciting feeling for me. I didn't know what life would throw at me during my drive: Flat tire, my car breaking down in the middle of my trip, running out of gas, all those things created anxiety. *I'm homeless. How much worse can it get?* I didn't care no more. My mind became numb to the world. Empty.

Mom had a lot of pills saved up from having breast cancer and other illnesses—everything from blood pressure meds to pain killers—all in one plastic bag, in the corner of her closet. I took it. It would be my backup if I didn't have enough money to travel back to Tennessee. I knew I could make some money off the pain meds. The scary part about all of it was that it could become the kryptonite that I would use on myself. If I used them then my life could be over without anyone truly knowing my whereabouts, or even caring for that matter, if things got too much for me.

I left behind everything that I owned. I figured I'd just go up there and come back with no problem. I had planned to leave that night, because I wanted to make it to Michigan in time to see the sunrise. Nashville, TN to Ann Arbor, Michigan in one drive would be a long trip, but with my determination and ambition, I was going to do it. I was locked in.

Before I crossed the state line, I wanted to make sure this was what I was going to do. *Yup! There's not going to be any other perfect time.* I thought. Once I had crossed over into Kentucky, there was no going back.

While traveling through Kentucky, the stars seem different. They were brighter and there were a lot more than back home. That was an amazing sight. Yes, it was dangerous sticking my head out the window to look up at the stars while driving. But I thought hey, what do I have to lose? My eyes were starting to get heavy. I needed to get to Ohio at least before I found somewhere to park for the night. I was still hundreds of miles away. My new checkpoint was the Indiana Welcome Center, where they have a rest stop. But my body was too exhausted to even make it to Indiana. I simply couldn't go another mile. I pulled over at a motel parking lot and slept there. I had the money to get a room for the night but doing that just wouldn't make sense since it was already past midnight and check out time was eleven in the morning. I only took a two-hour cat nap due to feeling so anxious about finally living out my desire. There was no chance of getting a comfortable night's sleep, so I hit the road again. A couple hours later, the sun began to rise.

It was very inspiring to travel through the different cities and see all the pretty landscapes. There were acres upon acres of rolling hills as far as my eyes could see. That right there gave me a sense that there are no boundaries how far you can go in this life. Only you can hold yourself back from the endless possibilities. Michigan was still hours away, but the scenery I was passing made time fly. The temperature was nice out, with a few clouds scattered about.

As I passed the huge expanses of land, I couldn't help but think how long it took the owners to accumulate it all. How much money do they currently have in their bank accounts? Who was the person that had the vision to start buying that property? How much money does it take to keep it maintained? Perhaps it was passed down, and all they had to do was put their name on it. Another one of my thoughts were generation after generation bought a little at a time and kept adding to it year after year. And, as time passed, their property grew to a larger scale and generated an abundance of wealth.

I always wanted to own a lot of land with rolling hills... though I don't know what I would use it for because farming is not the career for me. If anything, I would buy tobacco rights to it and lease it out. Other than that, it would be my own sanctuary. Some place I could go to escape from reality by sitting smack dab in the middle of one-hundred acres of rolling hills, surrounded by low green grass. That would be like heaven on earth. No children or screaming babies, no heavy traffic noise, no worries about finances, work, or any other major problems that would cause my mind to dwell on negativity. I'd have a few horses running around with God and I having a private moment, smoking on some of Colorado's finest cannabis. It would elevate me to sit right next to the Heavenly Father. *Matthew 7 (1-2).* And [I] don't think He wouldn't find anything wrong with it either by Him being a witness to me not abusing it.

As I was getting closer and closer to my destination, the clouds above were getting thicker. It was about to rain. *Noooo!* I was in Ohio now, and it wasn't looking pretty. I didn't check to see how the weather was going to be before I left. I was just going off pure luck that my whole trip would be nice. In some cities, it was cloudy with a tad bit of sunlight poking through. Then there were other parts where it looked like the rain was going to come down heavy. I was hoping and praying by the time I reached Michigan that all would be well. I stopped at a gas station to get a fill up and a couple of snacks. I had spent $60 to fill my Ford Explorer up to the top. One thing I noticed was that the further I traveled up north, the more expensive gas got. It sucked! All the money I had was on my debit card. I didn't check it, because I was too afraid to see my balance. If it was too low, it would put me in panic mode, and I would have to cancel my trip. Even though I was still hours away, I'd come too far to turn back now. If I had over $100 in my account, I was good.

While I was pumping gas I heard, "Go Ohio State!" and I knew Ohio fans were notorious for starting fights with Michigan fans. I was in full Michigan attire: Shirt, sweatpants, and a key chain. Since I was going to be on campus, I wanted to get the full experience as a Michigan college student. Hopefully, I could even sneak into some of the classes. I'm sure it wouldn't be the first time somebody tried it. The Ohio fan was cool. There was no animosity, and even if there was I wasn't about to take off my colors for no one. It turned out Michigan were at an away game to play Ohio State in college football. I had no clue. Now it made me want to represent them even more, since they had a game that same day.

Across the street was Bob Evans Restaurant. The fresh buttery bread smell that wafted over from the building was like heaven on earth. But I'm good with budgeting my finances, so even though I had enough money to get a small bite to eat there, I didn't. There still was a long drive ahead of me, and on top of that, I had to make it back home. While pumping my gas, I fantasized about eating there. As that fresh bread aroma filled my nose I smacked my lips. After I drove off, I opened the bag of chips and drink I bought from the store and let that satisfy me until my stomach *begged* for another bite to eat.

My mind began to venture to a strange place as I was driving… ideas of ending my life. I still loved the Lord and couldn't figure where these thoughts were coming from. I was going to check off one of the top three things on my bucket list, but after that, then what? I'd still be homeless, with no family, no *real* job, no friends, nothing. I would have to travel back in the make-believe realm of thought which was getting harder and harder for me as the days went by.

As I was driving on the bridge over the river, I thought about jumping out of my vehicle. That would be a Steve-O stunt! Then there were thoughts that came, while passing over an old creek, of parking my vehicle on the side of the road and walking off deep into the woods to overdose on Mom's pills. There were even thoughts about hanging myself under the creek bridge. It had to be somewhere that was secluded because I wanted my body to be beyond saving by resuscitation. My mind was beginning to play tricks on me. Thoughts like that only occurred when I was going over a bridge, or when I saw a creek. I would try to remember where all those locations were and would rank them to figure out which was the perfect spot. None of them were near Tennessee. I wanted to drop off the face of the earth. I was really in a dark place when I drove past those kinds of areas.

The moment had arrived! I was greeted upon entering the only state with two peninsulas. Welcome to Pure Michigan! It was partly cloudy with warm temperature. It didn't seem like it was going to rain. When I crossed into Ypsilanti, it was time to turn up. I was blasting my radio and celebrating as if I'd just won the Lottery. Ann Arbor was close, so I took the time to stop at the welcome center and browse around.

I threw my MapQuest papers in the trash and picked up a state map and some tourist attraction packets to get a feel of what it was like living there. I wondered how long it would take me to travel to the upper peninsula. I asked one of the workers in the shop.

"Oh, I'm not sure how long it will take. If I had to guess, it would be another twelve hours."

"For real?!"

"Yup, but that's just a wild guess."

He had asked another worker there how long it would take. She didn't have a clue either.

"Are y'all from Michigan?"

"Yeah, born and raised," he said.

"And you never been up there?"

"There's nothing there to do. Rarely you ever find people that want to travel there anyway. Where are you from?"

"I'm from Tennessee. I'm just passing through, about to check out the Michigan campus."

"I see you got on the colors. Are you going to the game later?"

"Naw."

"Well, enjoy your time here in Michigan."

"You can count on it."

I left and proceeded on my way. I wanted to go to the upper peninsula so bad, but I knew that was out of my reach. Even though I felt like there was no life for me back home except for the temp agency and my son—who I could no longer support due to my low income—it was too risky to go all the way up there just to say I'd experienced it and then turn back around. But being on the Michigan campus and sneaking into one of the classes to experience what being a student really felt like, that was all worthwhile to me.

I stopped at a gas station to buy a disposable camera to capture good memories, and noticed the gas reached an all-time high for me, at $4.99 per gallon for regular. It was good that I'd stopped for gas in Ohio when I did! I had taken a picture with a man that seemed like a die-heart Michigan fan as well. He had on the team attire because he knew that there was a game. By us being fans it was only right to take my first picture with him, and he agreed to it. Now it was time to head to my final destination. I pulled up on campus and just sat there, taking it all in. Now it was time for me to park my vehicle somewhere and go touring. I didn't realize how big the campus was. I thought it was just two or three big buildings, but the campus stretches on for blocks and blocks.

It truly was a sight to see. They had city buses with the school logo that covered them. It was something new that I never seen before. The first building I went into was the Michigan Union Hall. There were so many people going in and out of the building. There was a possibility that I could just slide right in without anyone noticing that I really wasn't a student. I sat around and thought about it… then I went through with my plan, because what else did I have to lose? Of course, I could get caught, but what's the worst that could happen? I'd only get told to leave the campus, it wasn't like I'd get arrested. The odds would work out in my favor.

That is one thing about me. If I put my mind to something, I will go all the way. It would be pointless to make that trip just to walk the streets. Naw, I wanted the full experience of giving myself my own personal tour inside and outside of the school and eating at one of the popular spots that fans go to on game days.

So there I was. I spent three to four hours going around, blending in with the other college students and not getting stopped by anyone. I toured around Ross School of Business. It was nice. I asked some of the college students that were sitting around in the lobby to take a picture with me. They seemed skeptical at first, and probably thought it was odd because they assumed that I also went to school there. I told them I was just browsing around, and they laughed when they found out I was doing my own tour. They gave me good words of encouragement about the school, and I was on my way without any of them calling for security.

As the day wore on, I noticed I wouldn't be able to tour around every campus that they had, so I drove over to the football stadium "The Big House" to take some pictures. I wanted to be back on the road by sunset. The entire day turned out to be hot and sunny. I thought about finding a spot to sleep and finishing up the next day, but that would be more money spent that I couldn't afford. Driving and walking around to different schools, interacting with the students by taking pictures with them, and eating at one of the popular spots. That was worth every risk of getting caught. I added up how much I spent when I got something to eat. All I knew was that my bank account still had at least $100 in it. It had cost me two full tanks to go from Tennessee to Michigan. And now that my trip was over, thoughts in my mind about picking a date and how I was going to end my life started to creep back up. My overall experience there was amazing, even though I didn't see everything. I was satisfied enough to scratch it off my bucket list and then back on the road I went.

My plan was to retrace my steps, because I didn't print off how to get from the school back home and I had thrown away the directions from MapQuest that I'd used to get there. *If I could just find my way back on the interstate, I'll be good,* I thought. I got a road map of Michigan while at the welcome center. That was my first time ever using a map like that. It looked like a small map, until you unfolded it several times. Then it covered half your body. I decided to go off memory. As I was driving, I noticed some places didn't look familiar to me. I had remembered, places will not look familiar unless I saw them over and over again. There was one spot I knew to remember to make sure I was on the right path.

I didn't see the landmark I pictured.. It wasn't that far away from the school. That I knew for sure. I kept driving, for some reason thinking it would soon pop up. Now an hour had gone by and there was a little bit of sunlight peeking over the horizon. I said to myself, *This can't be right. Ypsilanti isn't this damn far from the school.* I was now seeing signs that guided me towards Chicago… not Ohio. I pulled over and got directions from this lady at a gas station.

"I'm trying to head towards Ohio, and I don't know if I'm going in the right direction."

"Well, you're definitely not going in the right direction. You are going west, not south."

"You got to be kidding me! I knew something wasn't right when nothing looked the same, but I kept on going."

"Do you have GPS?"

"Naw. The paper I had to get up here, I threw away. The only thing I do have is a map of the state."

"Let me see it."

I went to my vehicle and pulled it out. She was a better navigator than I was. She told me where I was on the map, which I didn't have a clue about.

"You are right here, which is way out of your range. Where at in Ohio are you trying to get to?"

"I'm trying to get to Tennessee really, but once I made it to Ohio I was going to be on track. It was hours that I was heading straight without turning. And now I just wasted all my damn gas going in a different direction. *Fuck!*"

"Get back on the interstate and head in that direction," she said, pointing with her finger. "Then you will get to this point on the map which is the interstate you are talking about that you will have to travel for miles and miles."

"Cool."

"Are you going to be okay?"

"Yeah."

"All right then. Good luck."

"Thanks. I will need it."

I was screwed. It took me two full tanks to get to Michigan. With no GPS or any phone that could pull it up, it was hard to navigate where I was going.

I was so angry that after opening my vehicle door, I balled up the map and threw it on the passenger side. Now I know I should call to see how much money I had in my account. With all that wasted gas, I knew I was over budget, but still wanted to be stubborn and wait till the last option before I checked my account balance. There still was enough gas left to make it to Ohio, so I would at least be out of the state before it was time for a refill. I was furious with myself,

"Shit, shit, shit! I knew there was something wrong when I was starting to see different things than before. Why do I do stupid shit like that when I could have just fucking pulled over and asked for directions to make sure I was on the right track? Now I'm all the way out here when I could have been halfway to Ohio right now. Man, now I have to backtrack and then head down the right road. Fuuuuck!!!"

I pulled off, trying to get back on the right path before the sun tucked itself in behind the mountains. That wasn't going to happen. It seemed like you could hardly sit down in time to watch as the sun fell. That is how quick it went down.

Sometime later, I had seen where I took the wrong turn and couldn't help but laugh at myself. Being able to laugh at myself was the only thing that could keep me afloat at that very moment. I was trying to save what gas I had left by doing the speed limit. My gas was almost sitting on a quarter of a tank before I decided to pull over at an old coffee shop. I checked my map to make sure. I was still headed in the right direction. I had parked next to a custom black BMW convertible. That thang was nice, from the paint job all the way to the wheels and tires. My mind was in sudden panic when I thought about whether I could even make it to the next gas station, wherever that was. My destination was set on track. If I could just get the courage to check my account. Why was it so hard for me to check it? I couldn't tell you. All I knew is that if my account had less than what was required to get me back, I would have a nervous breakdown. At first, I really cared only a little bit if I made it back to Tennessee, but since I had checked off a major goal, I wanted to be back in my natural roots. A guy came out of the shop and asked if I had jumper cables. He wanted to know if I would jump start another guy's car. "The guy will pay you," he said. I quickly agreed to it. He went into the shop to find the guy that owned the BMW. The owner of the car came out.

"How the hell your battery die on you? This is a brand-new car!"

"I forgot my headlights were on. Do you have cables?"

"Yeah." I went to go get them. "Here."

He hooked up his ends on the battery terminals and I hooked up mine. His car was back up and running on the first start.

"Here, thank you for the jump start," he said, as he handed me some money. I was thinking it was maybe $10 or $15. I unfolded the bills. It was $60!

"It don't have to be this much," I said, handing some cash back.

"No, you take that. I was out here for a long time looking for someone that could jump me. I already called for a tow truck. Since we're out in the middle of nowhere, there's no telling how long it would take for them to get to me."

I wasn't going to tell him twice. That was a big sigh of relief. Right then, I knew God was still with me. What are the odds of you running into somebody so generous like that? Most of the time you don't receive anything for helping someone out like that, just a thank you and goodbye. We both were on our way. I stopped at the first gas station I saw and used the money to fill up my tank. My mind was deeply set on getting back home. My stomach didn't send any signals that it was starving, so there was no money spent on food. The last time I ate was a burger and fries that afternoon. I'm guessing the grease from the food delayed my hunger. Either that, or I was just so focused on making it back.

I felt myself getting sleepy as night came and the temperature started to drop. Even worse than that, the heater in my vehicle didn't work. My windows were starting to get foggy, and I knew it was best for me to find a spot to doze off for the night. I'd pushed my body to the limit where I couldn't fight off sleep anymore. Indiana was where I tapped out, in a Kroger parking lot. I got into my sleeping position. The only thing I had to keep me warm were the clothes on my back and my mother's blanket. That blanket was normally used for me to lay on for cushion, but the frost was too chilling to continue my normal sleep pattern. I put the blanket over the top of me and put my arms in my jacket. My shoes stayed on my feet while I curled up into a ball to maintain body warmth. I just need to close my eyes and soon enough I will doze off, I thought. "*Shit*! *It's getting even colder by the minute*." I would look at the time to see how long I'd been laying there while trying to doze off. When I felt I had laid there for at least an hour, I would get back up, check the time, and try to doze off again. Old man winter seemed like he was after me for vengeance.

My body began to shake from the frost clinging to my skin. My nose began to drip out snot that I couldn't manage anymore. My windows were covered with frost. *"How much longer can I stay like this? Fuck, fuck, fuck!"* I said with frustration. I was wide awake again. Sleeping was no longer an option. There was no point in staying there. I knew for a fact I wouldn't be able to rest. My only option was to continue, so that's what I did.

With the sleeve of my jacket, I tried to clear my front window to get a clear view of the road. No luck. No sooner than I got a clear view, the fog would creep back up the window. So I pulled a Jim Carrey stunt from the movie *Ace Ventura.* I drove down the road with my head out of the window! Imagine it's below thirty-two degrees and you're going fifty miles per hour down the road with your head hanging out the window, getting choked by the intense winds. It sucked! Better to be on a road and not the interstate. Every now and again I would pull my head in to step away from the potential frostbite. Good thing it was late at night, or else I would have gotten nothing but people pointing and laughing. I'm sure it would remind them of that movie, and they would be thinking that I'm doing it for attention. That was not for attention. That was for survival.

I was done with having to go back and forth on that map. I just needed easy and simple directions. I pulled over at a Tiger Market gas station and asked one of the cashier's how to get back to Nashville. A lady that was from Nashville gave me simple directions. The sun began to rise and, in no time, I was back in Tennessee where the weather was a lot warmer and the old way of navigation was over. I got my pictures developed at Walgreens. When I saw them, a permanent smile was embedded on my face. My trip had been a success.

CHAPTER 3
UNUSUAL TIMES

Labor Forcer started sending me out on long projects instead of daily tasks. The work would be either on a construction job or office cleaning. My hard work ethic never faltered, and that's why the clients kept requesting me to come back. The best job they sent me on was plumbing on a new construction supermarket project. No experience was needed for it, all I was doing was cutting and piecing the PVC pipe together. The condensation from the refrigeration system went to a drain which I ran pipe to.

That job lasted for months and it paid very well towards the end. They requested a lot of people, but some took the boss's kindness for weakness. He didn't scream or try to intimidate you by talking about firing anyone, and wouldn't give you a heavy workload. Our only job was to cut and piece together PVC pipe for the freezers. That is it. That got boring to me over time, so I asked if I could step up in the plumbing world and try something different. I was willing to do that even if there wasn't going to be a raise involved. He just couldn't do it. Some of the laborers that were called out there stayed on their phones even when we had work to do. Time after time they were told to put their phones away by other workers, or even the boss. I kept to myself and did not ask for help from the other laborers, even if I was struggling. It was my way of letting them fire themselves and guarantee I'd be the one who got a call back. That was my main tactic for securing the job. Sometimes, when they were on their phones a little too much, I would hint to them that the boss had a target on their heads. Their response would be, "So what? I will just go to another job," but they didn't understand that this was the best contract Labor Forcer had for us at the time. Luckily, he didn't stop requesting workers from my temp agency. I had a little to do with that. He had faith in me to last for the duration of the project.

I still had all the pills from Mom in my possession, and I wanted to profit from them. Another source of income was great! The pain meds were the start of my drug dealing phase. Never in my life had I sold any type of drug, and I could've never pictured myself doing it in the past. I was in my early twenties at the time. I was just going to sell what I could to make a little extra cash. Once the pill bottle was empty, then I would be done. No going back to refill on the prescription. That was the only way I could be sure I would not become addicted to them, or the fast money.

The fast life just wasn't for me. You get all that money to either have it taken, stolen from you, or you die behind it. Sure, you might hire people to do the dangerous work for you… but in the end one of them will snitch or turn against you due to jealousy. It's inevitable! I look forward to the *legal* high-class life, not the fast one. It's nice not having to live daily on pins and needles and be forever paranoid about the feds watching. Since I was new to the drug world, I had asked someone to see how much money I could make off just one pill. He said $20. In my mind, I thought, *I'm about to make a killing*. Mom had a lot of that particular kind. Twenty dollars just for one pill! And, on top of that, it would be 100% profit. I would have to stick to the code: Don't get high on your own supply. Now I can see how this drug game can become addictive, but my mind was programmed to get in the game and get out before I ever knew I was in it. What I mean by that is I would sell them in bulk, so I could get rid of them quickly instead of holding them for an extended period. All good things must come to an end. Now that I have the information needed to pursue my "desire" it was time to find some customers. How was I going to do that? I had no idea. I *absolutely* knew not to go parading around trying to look for anybody. I had to be quiet and subtle about it, so I could stay under the radar.

Back at the job, I was just working as usual when I overheard two employees talking about their drug habits. They were on some hardcore shit! Those two out-of-town workers were looking to get a quick fix to get high. Since they were from a different state, they didn't have the connections they once had back home. That was my opportunity to snatch them up as customers. I didn't want them to think I was a narc though, so I slid into their conversation smoothly. In the end, what I had was better than what they initially wanted. I went to my vehicle and handed both one pill. Their eyes grew big like it was a magic pill.

"Dude! Where did you get these?!"

"You know I can't tell you that. Can you work with it?"

"*Yeah!*" Both of them said together.

"They don't even make these anymore."

I'm not gonna lie. I felt like the man of the decade. What I had was very rare, and it was in my possession. They already knew how much it cost. Both darted in their pockets to see if they had enough.

"Man, we don't have enough, even if we did put our money together. Can you just take what we have, then later we will give you the rest? You can trust us. We all work together."

"Naw. I have to have the whole thing, but I will hold on to them for you."

Then they began to talk amongst each other trying to come up with a plan.

"What about you call your mom and have her Western Union it down here?" One guy said to the other.

"Look, it's close to lunch time, just give me what you have now and the rest by the end of the day. Here."

"For sure. I'm about to call my mom to send me some money down here now. You will have the rest for sure."

"Cool."

I was new to the game, and I didn't want to come out so harsh since they were my first customers. I had to maintain a good business relationship with them in order to keep their business. There were still plenty of pills left, which to their knowledge I had very few of, so if they never showed their face again it wouldn't hurt me. It was a matter of me testing their loyalty. After lunch break, he approached me with the rest of the money. From then on, I knew they were locked in.

I had officially become a street pharmacist. Since the pills were so expensive, they weren't coming to me on a daily basis and I wasn't gonna cut *anybody* no slack. They were on the job for no more than two weeks before they were sent on another project. So I made only a little money with them, but it was a start.

I occasionally had a drink, but wasn't into smoking or taking any type of over-the-counter pills for any reason until I hit rock bottom. Then I introduced myself to Black and Mild cigars. The sweet aroma that comes with it, you can't beat it. I experienced weed back in high school, only one time, but I didn't get any feeling from it. Mary Jane and I just wasn't meant to be. And on top of that, rolling up a blunt took skills which I didn't possess. Just a waste of money if you ask me. All my friends smoked, but I was a late bloomer. If I would have gone to them and asked for some, they would know something was not right. My situation was too sensitive to preach about. There were plenty of times, in the past, we all would be in a group and they would pass it to me, and I would always deliver it right back. My willpower was strong enough to be around it without being a consumer. Then, as time went on, they knew I just was not a fan of it. I didn't judge them, but it was something I was totally against.

At the time, being drunk was no different than being high. To me, both made you feel relaxed and I knew, that for others, it can trigger deep and dark emotions. Drinking was easier to access and less stressful because I could turn up the bottle and not have to worry about cops.

When it was time for me to head to a safe environment where I could park my vehicle and sleep for that night, I would tune into 92Q radio station, *The Quiet Storm*. By that time, I was in the "comfort" of my SUV, with a lit cigar in my hand and feeling ready to escape reality by listening to relaxing *soul* music. Smoking on that with good tunes in my ear made me feel like there were no worries. Maybe the cigar had something in it to make me feel numb to my world of pain. They always played good music, but this song by Deniece Williams called *Silly,* took me back to a place I was at in my relationship with Ladonna. Sometimes music does that. It transports you back to problems you've already gone through, or expresses problems you are currently going through and captures that mode of being in a relationship with that person.

I can relate to Silly, by Ms. Deniece Williams. In the end, we both were silly. It's one thing to share something with your boys, but it's another when you got that sweet lady you can hold on to while she kisses all over your neck. She would be rubbing her soft, soothing hands over your body to make you feel like a king. A man cannot be the rock all the time. Where does a rock go when it crumbles and breaks? It needs that special someone to talk to about how it once was, back before it cracked... how strong, mighty, and powerful it was. This gives it the strength to withstand the storms—which will come—and that very same rock can then stand tall in the middle and not budge.

Ladonna would be that lady for me sometimes. But only sometimes. I would be more likely to win the lottery than have her be there for me consistently, every time a situation occurred when I needed a shoulder to lean on. In my imagination, we were that powerful couple. But in reality? Yeah, in the real world, it was just the same ole *bullshit* we went through on a daily basis. All of that went out the window when my song came on.

♪♫ Silly of me to think that I could ever have you for my guy how I love you, how I want you, silly of me to think that you could ever really want me too, how I love you. You just a love around to score, I know that I should be looking for more, what could it be in you I see? What could it be? Oooh love, oh love, stop making a fool of me."

My next customer, who I will name Slick, introduced me to what I would call unusual times. He knew where to get any drug, but not mine. Slick was a friend of Ms. Spank, Ladonna's mom, so the majority of the time when I came over, he was there. I had inquired about his drug use through Ms. Spank; she knew what drugs he took, and didn't take. Slick wasn't a junkie. He was always well dressed and didn't show any type of drug addiction signs. He was just someone who likes a *good ole time* every once and a while. He seemed cool, so we became acquainted.

"You know about these right here?" I said, as I held up the pill bottle with just a few pills in it… I had most of them hidden in a baggie in my vehicle, since I didn't know if he would rob me or take off running with the product.

"*Yeah!* How much you want for 'em?"

"They go for $20 a pop."

"$20 per pill? Damnnnn! Why so much?"

"That's what they always went for. You can't find nobody that would sell them any cheaper."

He darted in his pockets and pulled out whatever he had: A plastic baggie with white residue in it, cash, and a blue lighter. He became embarrassed when I saw the baggie, but I looked past that. I was more focused on the cash. What he held in his hand wasn't near what I was asking.

"This all I got. Mess with me this one time."

"You can't go get more money?"

"Naw. We can make a trade." He reached in his pocket and pulled out the baggie.

"Here goes some crack rocks. That's an even trade."

Ms. Spank heard the conversation and immediately came from the kitchen to the living room to intervene. She knew what deal was going down already. She was the one that set it up, but she was totally against having crack in her house.

"Don't offer that boy that. What's wrong with you? And why you got that in my house?!"

"Oh, my bad. I didn't know I had it on me until I reached in my pocket."

"Naw. I'm far from doing that," I said.

"Come on, just let me get one to test it out. If it is what I think it is, I would definitely be back for more and have the right amount of money."

I thought to myself, this sucks not having enough clients to reject low ball offers and still feel okay about it. Well, guess it's part of the game to give away samples. Every person that wanted it, never had enough cash at the time.

"Mannnnn, give me all the cash you got and take this. This will be the only time it will happen." I gave him one and noticed how excited he was by him talking so fast.

"Will you be over Ms. Spank's house tomorrow?" He said.

"Yup, and around the same time."

"I will bring you the rest fo-sho. Thanks bruh."

"Aight."

In the mornings, I would drive to a convenience store before I went to work to wash up. Me spending time every morning in the restroom at the Labor Forcer office would make people suspicious about why I needed to go to the restroom first thing like that. And taking showers over at Ms. Spank's house began to get too embarrassing for me, so I had to move around. The gas stations with just one toilet were ideal. It would be simple to lock the door, and I could take my time unless someone knocked on the door wanting to get in. It wasn't exactly luxurious, but a bar of soap and a wash rag got the job done. My face and private parts were the main focus. If my arms were musty then I would get them too. Most of the gas station restrooms that I used had a lock on the door, which meant I could take my time to wash my whole body. As I washed up, the water would be going everywhere. I didn't care. I was in a rush. If a drain wasn't present, whoever's job it was to clean the restrooms would have to bring a mop and a bucket with them. In some restrooms there was a big puddle that I left behind from my bird bath. *Oops. Sorry.*

I hid my homelessness so good that you couldn't tell by looking at or talking to me. I would look just fine… but on the inside, I was dying. Dying of boredom, dying of not having someone to communicate with, dying of loneliness, and on top of that I was still arguing with Ladonna over any and everything. It was at this point that I noticed she was getting closer to this guy Mike. It was plain as day. She began to turn her back on me when I needed her the most. She wanted to detach from our relationship, which we desperately needed to do, but I was still clinging on to the greatness that appeared in my imagination. There was no doubt about it that I was tired of all the drama, but who else would spare their time to associate with me? No one. It used to be that after most arguments there would be make-up sex, which I thoroughly enjoyed any time of the day, but then that began to be too much for her. A hug followed by a slap on the ass is all I had in the way of affection from her. Not even no lip action or tongue wrestling.

I'm sure she would have no sympathy for me being homeless. It would be a deadly tool she would now have in her possession to use to "bury" me with shame. There were times in the past that I'd shared sensitive material with her. That information became the revenge tool she would pull out when we argued. Her words would cut me like a sword, bringing me down to my knees. An example is when I was suffering from my 3rd degree burns from the arson crime I pulled. *Both* of us were immature when it came to pushing each other's buttons though, so I can't pretend that I'm a saint when I used to do the same thing to her. We were tit for tat.

The next day, Slick met up with me at Ms. Spank's house. He gave me the rest of the money, and wanted to buy two more. Cool, I thought. Now this is the kind of guy I'm looking for. He would buy them once every blue moon, but I knew my clientele still had to increase. That's when it happened… people liked them so much that I decided to keep a few to see how much enjoyment such a small pill could bring. It had to be worthwhile, being that the street value was so high. So I tried one. I sat for a moment to see what would happen. No hallucinations, no scary thoughts, nothing that stimulated my mind, so I dozed off. That night, after I had smoked a couple of cigars while listening to 92Q, I was awakened from my coma-like sleep by a hard tap on my window.

"Who the hell is that?" *Tap! Tap! Tap!* "Who is it?" I didn't receive a response. The person's shadow went from the right side of my vehicle to the front, then to the left side. All my windows were iced over, and they were tinted also. I couldn't see shit. My mind was racing… who could it be? I hadn't harmed anyone, and I didn't owe anybody. Maybe I shouldn't respond, and they would go away. *Tap! Tap! Tap!*

"I'm in here! Who is it!"

"Can you let down your window buddy, so I can hear and see you better?" At this point it was either I follow orders or start up my car and get the hell out of dodge. But how was I going to manage to drive if *all* my windows were covered with ice. There was no point in running and leaving my vehicle behind when I hadn't done anything wrong. I gradually made my way from the back of my SUV to the front, where I could put the key in the ignition to turn it on. I cracked the front passenger window to see the person's face. It was a cop!

"Are you the only one in here?" he said, shining his high beam flashlight.

My body was exhausted. From waking up out of a peaceful sleep, to this, felt like I was getting mind-raped.

"Yeah." I said.

I lowered the passenger window all the way down to let him look and see I had nothing to hide. Well… almost nothing. He had asked for my license and registration and proceeded to tell me the reason he was there. I complied with the officer. It was a neighbor that called in a complaint about an SUV being in a church parking lot on numerous nights.

"Do you have anywhere else you can go?"

"No, I'm homeless." He could probably tell as much from all the junk that was in my possession.

He went to his car to run my records.

That's it. I'm done, I thought. *Well… I'mma experience what these other pain meds is all about. I will have to give them up anyway.* I took two at the same time and washed them down with some water left from an old bottle. I sat and waited patiently in the driver's seat for him to return. He got out of his car and started to walk towards my vehicle. I was thinking the car lot had called in on a stolen SUV, since I was still driving it with my payments being months behind.

My mind was racing… well, it's been nice. What mountain am I about to climb now? He will search my vehicle and find all of Mom's pills in here, which will get it towed with my stuff, and I would have to do some serious jail time, or even worse, prison*!*
He came to my passenger door. As he was glancing around one last time, he saw *all* the narcotics.

"Do those belong to you?"

"No. They're my mom's."
I went ahead and handed him the pharmacy bag that all the pill bottles were in. Didn't need them any longer for where I was headed. He looked through it.

"Janis McAdoo?"

"Yeah, that's my mom."
He knew the truth was being told when he had checked my ID and saw both of our last names matched.

"You better not be selling none of it," he said, as he handed me back the bag and my papers with ID, "you're good to go. For the night you can stay here, but tomorrow you will need to find somewhere else to sleep. I know you're homeless and all, but the neighbors don't feel safe with an unknown vehicle parked here night after night."

"Yes sir."

As he turned around and headed back to his squad car, I was in shock. My eyes were wide open and glued to him in astonishment. I watched him get in his car and leave. I asked myself "what, the fuck, just happened?" The early winter chills blew on me, so I rolled my window back up and sat there feeling stuck trying to snap back to reality. "Thank you God," I said. I took off my shoes prior to getting back into my cozy sleeping position and dozed off. The pills had no effect on me that I could tell. At the end of the alley was an open field where a house once stood, but it was demolished years ago. That was the new spot I chose to sleep, where I wouldn't be disturbed.

Time began to get rough. After the plumbing job, work began to decrease. I stayed on the job from start to finish and saved up some cash. All the laborers knew this would happen; it was a common thing during the winter season. The only thing Labor Forcer had that was steady was being a trashman. That was a job very few people liked, but not me. At least, not yet. Some days I would go to work at various locations, and other days I would sit at the office all day until the receptionist told us that was all the work for that day. Slick had stopped buying from me, so there was no extra income coming in from the pills.

Near the end of October, the nights seemed like they couldn't get any colder. After moving to a different spot to sleep, I once again had to adjust to the new environment. It was a dark area. The old spot had a streetlight close by, which put off just the right amount of light - not so bright it kept me up, and not so little that I couldn't see what was going on. This spot will have to do for now, I thought. I had only $5 to my name to make it to the next workday. Whenever that was. Two days had already passed with me not having any work. I thought, "*what can I eat that is cheap and will leave me satisfied? Micky Dee's!*" The McDonald's dollar menu was great for people trying to survive on a low income like myself. I found a way to make a five-dollar bill stretch. I would buy two 99 cent hamburgers; one for me in the afternoon between 1-3pm, and another for before bed which was at 10pm. No breakfast. I needed a way to make more money. Me selling any type of drug at the Labor Forcer office was a no-no in my book. Too many people would catch on, then I would be out of work, and possibly go to jail. Information gets passed around easily. I needed to stay quiet, so I wouldn't be bombarded with people asking or begging.

The plasma center was my only option. A couple of my coworkers told me about that place. To me, it was a place junkies go so they can get some money to satisfy their drug habit. I wasn't going to take a chance getting stuck with a dirty needle. But, as they kept explaining that it's not what I thought, I didn't care. Stubborn as I was, everything they said went in one ear and out the other. My finances were at an all-time low, and the gas in my vehicle was running out. I had to suck it up and check it out. My first time going in there wasn't what I thought it would be. It was full of people who'd just fallen on tough times and needed a little extra cash to survive. The place was clean, and the people were friendly. I went through the process of getting checked in. When it was my turn to withdraw my blood plasma, they put me in a room and started the procedure. The machine began to act funny. The nurse rechecked all the procedures to make sure she had hooked me up to the machine correctly. "Everything I did is right," she said. This nurse was new, and never encountered a problem like this. With the needle in my arm pumping out my blood and the machine having technical difficulties, I began to get nervous. As my blood started to drip into the clear bag, I saw that it was dark. It was going at a slower pace than usual, which is why the nurse got the doctor. *Beep! Beep! Beep!* A couple of lights on the machine came on.

"What's going on nurse?"

"I don't know, I'm doing everything right."

"Oh Lord. Is it me or the machine?

"Let me get another nurse over here. Hang on."

"I knew I shouldn't have come here."

She went and grabbed the doctor, who had plenty of years in the field. Immediately upon her arrival she knew the solution to my problem.

"There's nothing wrong with the machine. It's doing its job to let us know your blood is too thick to process. The reason your blood is so dark and thick could be because you haven't eaten much or drunk a lot of water, or both."

"Yup, that makes sense to me," I said.

I was fine. She had explained to me that I needed to eat more and drink plenty of water at least two days before coming back. As for that moment, there was nothing anyone could do. She had to take me off the machine. I was appreciative that it wasn't anything life threatening. The only thing that kept me from dying of starvation was the two McDonald burgers I was eating every day, one in the afternoon and one before bed. I was called out on a couple of jobs since then, but still tried to conserve my money by shopping off the dollar menu. The next time I went to the plasma center, it went well. I had followed orders and was in and out in no time, and on top of that I received two payments; one for my first visit of being hooked up to the machine, even though I didn't donate any plasma, and the other payment for the visit that day. Putting $30 in my pocket just for donating plasma was fine by me. You could visit two to three times per week and make at least $15 for each visit. This was now my new source of *guaranteed* income. Only I could stop the money coming in from that source, which was something I didn't intend on doing. And when I told the guys on the job about my experience, their comment was "See, I told you so." With extra cash in my pocket, I went out of my way to buy some snacks so I wouldn't have to eat out all the time. Food stamps were on my mind, but if I signed up for them, it would go to Kiesha's address and I didn't have a way of getting it without using her key to open the mailbox. Right when everything was starting to run smoothly, life, yet again, hit me with an unexpected uppercut. Down I went.

Two weeks hadn't even passed before I was told to move from the new spot where I was sleeping. It was the middle of the night when I was, once again, woken up by a bright flashlight and an officer tapping on the window trying to get me to roll it down. Like always, I complied, since I didn't want to be in any more trouble than I already was in. But this time, I made sure the pills were hidden prior to me letting down the window. This cop was cool. He didn't ask me for identification, insurance, or registration papers. He simply told me to find another spot. The neighbors—who I wasn't bothering, *at all*—had called in a complaint and therefore the cops had to come out and do their job. I needed a spot where it would be okay to rest and not have neighbors complain. Everywhere that I tried to rest, it seemed like the neighbors were out to get me. There I was, a homeless man just trying to make it through the night, and people couldn't let me be. There would always be police telling me to fucking move.

I was stuck on where to go next. In addition to that, it was in the early hours of the morning. I was trying to think of a perfect spot where I could finally sleep there for however long it would take to get back on my feet. Somewhere I would not have to worry about being woken by a cop. I drove around for thirty minutes and realized there was no such place. I would have to get in where I fit in, and look forward to the day where I'd be woken up out of my sleep again.

Since I had a lot of pills left, I decided to make the trade with Slick. Give a pill for $20 worth of crack rock. I simply could not go another inch. No matter how hard I tried to get on the right track and stay there. Something or someone always reminded me that I wasn't shit because I was homeless. I was really starting to experience the emotions homeless people go through.

Some of them don't talk to themselves because they're crazy. They do it because no one else will have a conversation with them. Therefore, they turn to their own imagination and feelings and let it just pour out of their body, unfiltered. I began to feel that way. But I would never claim the title of being crazy. Homeless yes, but *crazy* wasn't in my vocabulary. Everybody has done something crazy in their past, but that doesn't define that person as being crazy. We all are human, therefore we make mistakes.

Ms. Spank set up the meeting again with Slick and I. She didn't know what really was about to happen, she thought of it as just another drug deal. But this time I wasn't myself. My body began to slip into the dark hole of depression. He didn't have the crack on him when we met, so he went to get some and outside the house is where we made the trade. One pill for $20 worth of crack. At first, I thought I was being cheated by the small amount he gave. I didn't realize this was a rich man's drug. In other words, only the rich can afford the addiction.

The deal was a success. It felt weird having it. This was the first time I would ever try something of this caliber. Fuck it. I had it, and there was no such thing as a trade back or refund in this game. You get what you get, and that is final. My intentions weren't to take it right away. I needed to be in a safe place, not around people, in case it took control of me. I kept it in the sun visor of my vehicle. I was going to snort it, but just had to wait until the time was right… when I had reached the point of no return. And that's how Slick introduced me to what I call, unusual times.

CHAPTER 4
COLLEGE GRADUATION

My friendship with Tracy grew stronger as I hoped it would. She would take $10 to braid my hair, but I decided to be a little bit more generous and started paying her $15. That was the average cost. Her work was fast and neat. It got to the point where she was letting me come over to her house and not have to meet at Ms. Spank's. There were many times I wanted to ask her out but didn't. I didn't have the balls. The time wasn't right. We only known each other for a month. Our normal conversations, when she was doing my hair, would just be about whatever we were watching on TV or whatever drama that happened recently around the hood. She lived in the projects. When you live there, you hope and pray you don't get that announcement that your loved one has been shot, killed, or incarcerated. Tre-Tre, my son, lived in the projects as well. That is where I spent the majority of my free time until it was time for me to find an abandoned spot to sleep for the night. That's where I played basketball and watched fights, between teenagers mostly. My goal was to get him out of there, but how would I do that? My own circumstances weren't the best. Seeing him in that environment, where gunshots and police sirens were common, was hard.

I never lived in the projects, but where I'm from might as well have been. People would all the time shoot their guns in the air across the street from where I once lived with Mom, and constantly blast their music late at night when everyone was trying to go to bed. Down on Lewis Street was *bad,* with prostitutes walking up and down. But they never did mess with me or my friends as we passed through. Guess they had more respect for the kids than they do themselves. Police stayed close by, because either people would frequently call about some complaint, or there was a serious matter that needed to be addressed in the neighborhood. My friend once found a dead body in a dumpster on Lewis Street. He told his mom, and she called the cops. He told me he had walked by the dumpster and smelled something strange. He'd peeked his head over in the dumpster and there it was… a lifeless Black male. *Dead!*

There was another moment where everybody was on the basketball court and one guy passed straight through our game. We could tell something happened, or was about to happen, by the look on his face and his pace. Oh well, let the game continue, we thought. Seconds later, another guy came running through with a blue bandana tied around his upper and lower face. Only his eyes were visible. He had shorts on, no shirt, and tattoos covered the top half of his body. We already knew he was on a mission. We didn't realize the severity of it because it is a gang hood. Most people around that way wore blue bandanas, whether they were affiliated or not. That was normal, but what wasn't was that he had a gun in one hand and was trying to run while he held up his shorts with the other. Everybody knew this was going to be a murder case, and we all knew we did not want to be witnesses. I don't care what the cops tell you… word will get around that you snitched, and your head will be on a chopping block. It sucks, but that's the code we lived by in the hood. With all our eyes wide open, we froze. *Pow! Pow! Pow! Bang! Bang! Pow!*

Everybody grabbed what they came to the court with and ran in the opposite direction of the shooting. We were all terrified of getting hit by a stray bullet. As we ran through the projects yelling, "*Dey shooting! Dey shooting!*" people that were sitting on their porches now ran into their houses. Most of us split up during the run. I ended up on a guy's porch I had been playing ball with. We looked around to see if they were coming back in our direction and stayed put until the coast was clear. My vehicle was parked right where all the action was. My life is more important than me trying to dodge bullets just to get in my vehicle and leave. Everyone regrouped at his place. After the sirens had died down, we waited ten to twenty minutes before we went anywhere. When we were sure the danger was gone, everything went back to normal as if nothing happened. No one knew if someone had gotten shot or died, we would just have to tune into the nightly news to find out. That was life in the Southwest Projects.

Parents let their kids run about outside, playing with their friends, just as long as they were in the vicinity where they can hear their name being called. Tracy's kid and mine played together sometimes. Her son is four years older than mine, but that didn't stop them from kicking the ball around, or riding scooters together, which was great! Now it wouldn't be so hard for me to weasel my way in to ask her out. We held great conversations when she was doing my hair, and our sons were getting along well. It wouldn't be long before I popped the question. I just needed a little bit more time. She told me that she didn't want to have another child after the one she was carrying was born. To my knowledge, she was fed up with having babies by "lil boys" who would not step up to take responsibility as a man should. Tracy even told me she was willing to give her current baby daddy another shot at raising their child together after he had cheated on her during pregnancy.

"He still wanted to be a player," she said, "And for that reason, I'm not having any more kids. Once my baby is born, I will get my tubes clipped and burned. I will not take the chance of getting them tied. There are stories of people that tried that method and their tubes became untied, resulting in an unplanned pregnancy. I don't want dem kind of surprises."

She was finished having kids, but I was not. If we were a couple, there would be all boys and no girls. I at least wanted to have a girl in the mix.

"What if the next person you date wants to have another kid?" I asked.

"Nope! Not happening."

"Don't you want a little girl?"

"That's what I was hoping for when I had this one, but as you know, it didn't turn out that way."

"What about adopting one? That's always been in my thought process. If my next child is a boy, or the lady that I meet don't have a girl and can no longer get pregnant, then I definitely will adopt one."

"That's a thought, but that's much later on down the road."

Life really must be hard for her. Here she was, about to have her second child, and neither of those children's fathers were around. Her first-born's dad took care of him from a distance. He had everything he wanted, but the second was a bum. The first time I saw him was when she did my hair on her porch. She pointed and said,

"There go my bitch ass baby daddy right there." He never come by. He don't even check on me to see how my pregnancy is going, but that's cool. I'mma be alright."

I knew not to intervene. These are family problems, and I don't hold a candle to Dr. Phil when it comes to counseling relationship issues! I would be her sounding board, so she could vent out all her frustrations. Hopefully, all her frustrations would be over when we became a power couple. She never did talk about him much, really, there was nothing much to talk about. As for me, I didn't look at her current situation, I looked at the person she would become. She worked until she couldn't, took care of her kid, was a good provider, a protector, and independent. Wherever she had to go, she would walk or ride the bus, and didn't consume anything that would damage her lungs. Even though she couldn't work due to her pregnancy, that didn't stop her from earning money. Her money maker was doing hair on the side. I looked past the project situation and the two kids. Not everybody in the projects wants the easy way out by living on government assistance. Some people had a hardship in their life, and this was the only option they had left.

I even made an attempt to apply for one, but every time I went, either the office was closed, or something distracted me from going. In the long run, I found sleeping in my vehicle to be better than the projects. If some peace and quiet was needed, I could find a vacant spot and rest there. I didn't have to worry about anyone breaking into my vehicle, because most of the time I was in it.

Ladonna had moved out of her place and was now living back with her mom. All I knew was that she was close to Tracy, who I was trying to embrace. I was scared that Tracy would notice her behavior and then that would be a wrap for me. No more doing my hair, no more chilling with her, *nothing!* At that point, Ladonna and I were friends with benefits. Mike was starting to come around more and more. I caught on quick, and tried not to think about it, but he was an alcoholic. If he was around her then that meant he was also around my son. Nothing ever comes good with an alcoholic. There was nothing I could do. But it was not my house that he was coming over, so I couldn't tell him not to come back. Ladonna wasn't in a serious relationship with me, so I couldn't tell him not to talk to her anymore either. And even if I did, she would still communicate with him anyway. But what I could do, was tell him not to cause any harm to my son, verbally or physically, which he already knew. There were some jealousy issues there that I can admit to. I should not even be that way, but I still needed someone in case Tracy shot down my offer of being my girlfriend. We were talking, but it still wasn't official.

There's something about having a crazy argument—where veins are popping out of your neck—then immediately having sex right after, that Ladonna and I both enjoyed. Don't know what it is, but the sex would be ten times better. When I surrendered my side of the argument, I would force a kiss on her lips and around her neck, then whisper in her ear very seductively,

"I'm sorry baby. I love you. You're right."

She would still try to push me away like she was mad. Then she'd turned around. That was my cue to get behind her. At that point, my dick would be at full attention. I would press it on her butt and firmly grip her waist with my hands while gently kissing on her cheek.

"Mooooove. You need to stop," she'd say, while at the same time giggling, "I'm still mad at you."

Then I would nibble on her neck to get her to stop playing games. She wanted it just as bad as I did. As I slowly moved my hands up to start massaging her perfect breasts, she would jerk away and find something miscellaneous to do. But I'd be persistent, and there was a "situation" arousing that needed taking care of. Immediately! I would be too close to the real thing to settle for a hand job. "Can I have a hug? *Please,*" I'd ask. Every woman knows when a guy asks for a hug after trying to seduce her what his intentions really are. And it has nothing to do with feeling sorry. She would turn to face me, put her arms around my neck, and our lips would meet. I would pick her up with her legs straddled around my waist and her arms locked tight around my neck. That's when the tongue wrestling and fireworks would begin. It didn't matter what room we were in at the time: Kitchen, hallway, bathroom, living room, wherever! It would go down, just as long as my son wasn't around. If he was there, then the lustful show would be moved to a private area such as the bedroom.

It wasn't all the time that our arguments ended like that though. Sometimes, the police would be called, and I'd be locked up for minor issues. And then there were times where I needed to be put behind bars due to my actions. And, like a dummy, I would always find my way back to her. I didn't want Mike to experience what I was experiencing when it came to making love. I don't think he got the tools to change her attitude the way that I did when a heated argument transformed into wonderful foreplay, which led to incredible sex. In my eyes, he would *never* experience sex like Ladonna and I did. He was cool with Ms. Spank, because her oldest son and him grew up together. But her oldest son stayed across town, and I know he wasn't over there to visit Ms. Spank like he tried to show. He kept coming over. The more he came over, the less Ladonna wanted to deal with me. At the same time, it was pushing me even more to ask Tracy to be my girlfriend. The thought of being rejected was still too devastating for me though. I remained in the friend zone for a moment longer than expected.

I had forgotten the date of my college graduation. I thought for sure that after all this time it already had passed. Unclear of the circumstances, I needed to go and check to give me some peace of mind. If it already had passed, it would suck, but I wouldn't be too upset about it because it wasn't like my family was going to be there anyway. At least I didn't expect them to be. We were still going through some issues, and the main part of it was getting the award to show proof, to myself, of how far I had come. I went to the school to talk with the receptionist at the front desk and, to my surprise, it was only days away. I had caught them just in time. She handed me my robe, hat, and gold tassel (for being on the Dean's List multiple times) and told me the time and location of the ceremony.

I could have taken a bird bath in a convenience store like I would normally, but this was different. I got a motel room for a graduation present to myself. Now I could clean up and look nice for my big day. I took everything back to the motel, laid it out on the bed, and took pictures of it. It amazed me that I still would be attending my graduation after all the struggles life had put me through. Now it was a matter of whether or not I should tell my family, or just attend it alone. If I did tell them and they became too busy to show up or just didn't want to go, that would hurt tremendously. On the other hand, if I did tell them and they actually showed, then it would be a plus. I hadn't talked to my family for a while at that point and didn't know if there was still animosity in the air or if it was all behind us. It would be cool to have my family in the audience cheering me on, and to not feel left out as the only person on stage who didn't have any family support. Whatever decision I made, it had to be made quick. My ceremony was right around the corner, and if I didn't give them enough time to make arrangements for it then it would be on me.

The big day had arrived! Everybody was excited to end this chapter in their life and start a new chapter in their chosen fields. The ceremony was held in a massive church. There were only a few people that I had class with that attended. The other students dropped out of school or took some semesters off. I was ready to get my award that I'd worked extremely hard for since the beginning. Before the presentation began, everybody went around chit-chatting with friends. It felt good. It was now time to go into the auditorium where the main event was going to take place. Just like high school graduation, as you walked into the door you heard pomp and circumstance by: Edward Elgar played over the loudspeakers. There was good energy that filled the room as we, graduates of 2012, entered.

Since it wasn't many of us that graduated, we all sat on the stage instead of in the seats below like you would normally see. I thought that was odd, but being that this was a technical college and not a university, it made sense. My plan was to pay off all the student loan debt. After that, I'd go back for nine more months for my associates degree. Instead of taking out another loan, which would put me back in debt, my plan was to pay my way through with cash. It cost me $15,000 for a tech college diploma. There was information out there for scholarships and grants, but the only blessing that I received was my Pell Grant, same as everyone else who comes from a low-income household. I applied for many scholarships and got none. Oh well, it's part of the norm when you attend college. Was it worth being in that much debt for a piece of paper? I didn't have an answer at that time.

One by one, each graduate went to the front and center of the stage to receive their award. Each of their loved ones stood up and cheered. I looked out across the crowd and saw no one was out there to cheer for me. At first it didn't bother me, but depression slowly started to creep in. When each person's name was being called all you heard was loud screams, and "I'm so proud of you! You did it. Yayyyy!" As for me, I knew people would clap to show respect to all graduates, but dammit I wanted the same treatment as the other folks. I began to get choked up. Then I heard my name called, "Terrance McAdoo." A few people clapped. It was mostly the staff members that worked at the school, but I appreciated it. At least somebody acknowledged my success. I smiled as I went to the front to get my diploma, but it quickly vanished when I returned to my spot to wait while others received theirs. After the graduation, I went straight back to my room to take in what I'd just experienced.

I was too scared of the response that I would have received from my family to ask them to attend. In my head, asking them would mean nothing but rejections from everyone except for Keisha. She is the type to forgive quicker than the others, but still I was unsure and didn't want it to backfire. I hadn't been in touch with them in a while, and me calling out the blue like that to ask for their support didn't sit well with me. So I went through it alone, just like I did with everything else.

CHAPTER 5
CRACK IS A POWERFUL DRUG!

After getting kicked out of my sleeping spot for the second time, I was realizing that was how it was going to go. Right when I started to get nestled in my space, someone would ask me to move and I'd have to go back on a scavenger hunt to find the next spot to sleep. My *new* location was at the end of Lewis Street, outside some run-down duplexes, in an area which had gotten much better than it was when I was a kid. No prostitutes, no dope boys. There were only enough parking spaces for the residents who lived there, but I always grabbed an open spot. If they told me to move, then so be it, but for now that is where I laid. The first night was a success. No one questioned where I came from and why I was taking parking spots from people that lived there. I knew that wouldn't last long though. So, based on my previous experience, I was already on the hunt for the next spot to sleep and was hoping to find one closer to my job.

One day, Ladonna wanted to spend some time with me. She knew about the story I'd brought up about my "uncle" having no running water, but this time I told her he had water, but that his lights were cut off, so we couldn't go over there. "It's cold in my uncle's house, and it's cold out here, so we might as well try something more spontaneous by sleeping in my truck," I said. She grabbed her covers and a pillow, and we went to Lewis Street where I set up a place to sleep. Every time I went there, I made sure it was around 10:00 pm. That way I was certain all the residents would be in their houses. If there was an open parking place, it was available for me. We got snuggled in, with my back seats down for extra leg room. I sparked up a conversation,

"What's going on with you and Mike?"

"Nothing."

"Don't seem like nothing. Why is he coming over more and more now?"

"I don't know. I'm tired, let's just go to sleep."

I was egging her on and on about the situation. And she was steadily trying to avoid it. It was a topic that really *didn't* need to be discussed though, because if she had told the truth—that they were talking—it wouldn't stop me from trying to see her. The more I tried to squeeze information out of her, the more she threatened to leave. It was clear she wasn't going to sit and talk about her and Mike's friendship. She had reached her breaking point.

"Take me home."

"Okay, we don't have to talk about it anymore."

"No. I want to go home now, or I will walk!"

This seemed like mind games to me, and I wanted to call her bluff.

"Well, there's the door."

She started to get her things.

"I'm sorry," I said, as I tried to kiss her, but she'd clearly had enough and there was no coming back.

I dropped her off in her neighborhood. She left her covers in the vehicle, which I *desperately needed.* It was extremely cold that night. After I drove back to my spot, that's when it all hit me. It was my fault she was mad. At first, I couldn't understand why she wouldn't answer my questions about him. It was me looking for an argument, which she could sense, because what difference would it make if she did? We still were going to stay in touch like we had always done after a heated argument.

That's when I reached into my sun visor and pulled out the crack. I knew this white substance had people going crazy back in the 80's. How can something so little be worth so much? It felt like I was holding an atomic bomb in my hand. One hit and I could be hooked. That would be my first time trying this drug. Paranoia gave me a visit, as I looked around to see if anyone was watching. My eyes would stare out the window, then back at the drug, then back out the window. I began to study it like it was a science experiment. I smelled it—it was odorless—as I took it out of the bag and looked at it closely. I said to myself, "damn. I should have known that wasn't an even trade and said something. I remember I used to talk about the crackheads, and now I'm about to become one. Whatever. I have nothing else to lose." I laid it on my center console and took out my ID to crush it up, just like I've seen in movies. After taking my time to make sure it was crushed up fine, it was time for business. With one finger on my nostril and the other nostril open, I took a long hard sniff and cleared it with one go. There was still a pinch of it in the plastic bag. I shoved the whole bag in my nose.

"The damage has been done. I'm gonna sit here and chill and wait to see what happens."

It was cold, so my mind was more focused on the weather than the drug. Then I noticed I had been stuck staring out of the window for a long time and hadn't realized it. In the rearview mirror, I could see my eyes were *wide* open. I wouldn't have noticed if I hadn't looked. I was starting to get scared because I couldn't stop my eyes from being that way. Music would calm me down and take my mind off the drug, I thought. I turned on the radio and my head began to bounce up and down, up and down. My body began to dance uncontrollably.

"This must be Grade A crack. I'm dancing to music I don't even like. And now, this is the best music I've heard! This is crazy!" I tried to repeat some of the lyrics, but my mind was thinking faster than I could get the words out and causing me to stutter. There was no way of getting a single sentence out, no matter how hard I tried. I had turned up the music to the max. And I was having my own little concert in my vehicle, during an extremely cold evening with no one watching.

I dared myself to take it a step further. I reached into the bag of pills. My curiosity wanted to test out a different prescription this time. There was a half-cut plastic water bottle that I used for an ashtray. I had some water in it, so the cigar ashes wouldn't burn through the bottle. I took a pill and drank a little bit of the ashtray water. Seconds later, I threw it back up. It started to get difficult to say words.

"Shit t-t-that's nasty." But I was determined to get this pill down. I tried to get down another one of the same kind by drinking some more garbage water, and again, threw it back up. "W-w-w-well that p-pill is not cooooooooperating. L-let me just wear off the c-c-coke f-f-f-f-first." It was a weird feeling. I was excited and scared at the same time. My plan was to go to work the next day. I thought the effects would be gone by then.

The next morning, my eyes were still buck wide open. I thought, *if I practice keeping my eyes at the normal level, then I'll be cool.* My stuttering problem was gone, but that problem had been replaced by a new problem. My vision was blurry. My gas tank was near empty, so I decided to go to the gas station up the street to fill up. I had to focus on the road, and when thoughts came to my head I'd push them to the side. My thoughts were trying to distract me from paying attention to the road, but I managed to reach my destination unharmed. The challenge I then faced was that I could not hide being high. If I couldn't pretend to act normal, people that could see me would automatically know what type of drug I took. Crack, that I know of, is the only drug that will make your eyes like that.

I tried using my debit card at the gas pump so no one would notice my flaw. The card reader kept declining my payment. *There must be something wrong with this reader,* I thought Now it was time for me to act normal and pay inside the store, where other people were. I made it to the sidewalk at the entrance of the store. I couldn't figure out how to get both of my own feet up and on the sidewalk if my life depended on it. By my experience, I knew the drug still had control of my mind. This was something so simple, but I still couldn't do it. There were a couple of people outside of the store watching me trying to accomplish getting on the sidewalk. I didn't see them at first, until I overheard their conversation,

"Aye y'all! Look at him over there!"

"What's wrong with him?"

"That mane tweaking supaaaa hard."

Right then I snapped back and conquered the sidewalk. As I was about to go in the door, a guy stared me straight in the eyes, like he knew what I took, and that was the final straw of me acting. I couldn't control this. No matter how hard I tried. This took control of my mind, body, appetite, *everything!*

"Mannnn I'm zooted," I said. Instantly, one of the guys started laughing hard and loud. As I grabbed the door handle and was about to walk in the store, a guy in his car yelled out,

"Crack is a powerful drug!"

He wasn't lying. I tried to get $20 worth of gas. The first time I swiped my card, I put in the wrong pin number. The cashier reset the screen. The second time, my card came back *declined.* "Let me try $15," I said. At this point, customers were starting to pile up behind me. After my third attempt of trying to use my card, it came back declined again! I left the store feeling embarrassed. Being strung out on crack and not having even $20 to my name was a wake-up call. I wasn't going to the plasma center often, but then I knew I needed to start going on a regular basis. I got in my vehicle and left, feeling disgusted with myself. On the bright side, I avoided being the laughingstock at work. This happened for a reason. If I'd had $20 to make it to work, I absolutely would have gone. This embarrassing situation at least stopped me from feeling worse than I would've felt if I had shown up at work, coked out of my mind.

By the afternoon, nothing had changed. I didn't know how long my eyes were going to stay like that. It's not something that you can sleep off and be fine when you wake up. I drove over to Ms. Spank's home and located Ladonna in her bedroom. I told her about me taking the drug. She was more worried than disgusted. She knew it's an easy drug to get hooked on, and didn't want me to go down that road. She asked a lot of questions. Some she knew the answer to and some she didn't.

"Are you okay? Do you want me to call the ambulance?"

"Naw, I'm good."

And then my heart began to race and my breathing got really heavy. She jumped off the bed and ran to get Ms. Spank.

"Do you need me to call you an ambulance, Terrance?" Ms. Spank asked.

"No."

It didn't feel like a life-or-death moment for me, it was just another circumstance that was uncontrollable. My appetite had faded away. The food that I usually ate didn't taste the same. All day long I went without eating, and didn't have the desire to. What I tried to eat tasted like cardboard. Any other time this would be a huge embarrassment. But right then, I clearly didn't *care* what people thought about me, or if they looked at me different. I was going through a dark season in my life. To my understanding, we all have skeletons in our closet. Some people know how to keep them tucked away, others try to fight them, but they always get revealed. Then there's people who have accepted their flaws and are not afraid to talk about them to other people, so they can learn from their mistakes and not make the same ones. I was the one who was trying to fight it. I was struggling to keep it all tucked in.

By the end of the night, most of my mind came back to me. I could eat regular foods again, and my vision wasn't blurry anymore. The only thing left to recover were my eyes. Ladonna said it was scary to see me like that. Never in a million years did she think this would be something that I would've tried. I couldn't agree more. I gave myself a lame excuse to try it because of my situation. I was slowly losing grip on life, so therefore it turned me into a daredevil. It took two whole days for my body to return to its original state.

CRACK IS A POWERFUL DRUG!

Back at Lewis Street, people were starting to notice my vehicle being in the parking lot. There were a few stares during the day when I would sit there to waste time. I was certain they would ask me to move. It was only a matter of time until that happened, and I was ready. My friend's aunt lived in the duplexes there. She saw me many times sitting there in my vehicle, but never confronted me. That was, until one day when I waved at her. Then she finally came over to see what was going on. Again, I gave only a brief description of my situation,

"I'm homeless, just looking for a place to sleep." She thought I looked familiar, but wasn't sure. She was okay with it, and passed the word around to her neighbors. She left me alone and continued on her way. I thought, *finally, a place where I can spend my nights and not have to worry about being asked to move. This is where I'm going to be for a while thank God.*

There were times when I would give people rides for money that were living in that area. No big deal. At most, they would give me $10. To me it didn't matter. Any money is better than having no money at all. We were helping each other out, and that was much appreciated by all. They weren't charging me rent for taking up one of their parking spaces, which was a plus. This one lady started to abuse my kindness. I didn't mind giving rides, but doing it all through the night till the wee hours in the morning was too much. My body still had to get some rest for work the next day. In her mind, that didn't matter. "Give me a ride right now, or find you somewhere else to sleep." It was late at night when I was woken out of my sleep. Soon, I realized that it was a piece of her property that I was holding. It would be wrong for me to turn her down and still expect to park there. After all, she was paying me gas money, so I took her and her friend up the street. Night after night, I was woken up by people who were desperately needing to be somewhere late at night. I simply couldn't handle the pressure anymore. I thought long and hard about leaving or staying. If I stayed, people wouldn't respect my sleeping hours and would wake me up all night. If I left, that's easy money that I wouldn't get anymore. This time there was no one that told me to move, I took the initiative and did it myself. I disappeared from that location without ever returning. I could replace the easy money by donating my plasma on a regular basis. That was how I finally felt secure in making the decision to leave.

The next location was a Piggly Wiggly parking lot. They never had a lot of customers during store hours. Finding a new location from where I currently was staying became a new habit. If or when I was told that I could no longer park there, my next stay would be at Kroger. It was right down the road from where I was at. Store parking lots were my main attraction from then on. My choice of store had to be one that was big enough that they wouldn't notice my vehicle being there night after night. If even on their busiest days they still had empty spaces, that was a good sign. Then I knew a space would be available for me every time. Piggly Wiggly and Kroger fit that criteria, and both were right down the street from Labor Forcer.

Instead of washing up at different convenience stores, Kroger then became my place to take a birdbath in the mornings. Piggly Wiggly would still be closer when it was time for me to go to work, but Kroger was suitable for me at that moment. Prepared with a washcloth, soap, rag, toothbrush, and a travel size tube of toothpaste all in a baggie that fit in my big coat, I would head into their restroom, making sure no one else was in there with me. Checking under the stalls to make sure there were no feet gave me confidence that I was all alone. It would be like a drive-thru car wash, get in and get out. It was a multi-person restroom, so there wasn't a lock on the entrance. At any moment, somebody could have walked in. There was always a fear that I would be caught standing in the mirror shirtless, with soap suds under my arms. I washed my face first, then the other parts of my body that would get dirty or smelly.

The only close encounter that I had was when a guy walked in on me brushing my teeth. That was not that embarrassing for me, but it still felt awkward. Thank God it was after I had washed under my arms. It would always be very tempting to grab a snack size bite to eat and walk around, pretending like I was grocery shopping. That never happened though, because if I did get caught then I was scared they would ban me from all Kroger locations. *Forever!* I was always conscious of being seen on the cameras. Me going in the store with a big black coat on and walking straight to the restroom every morning and leaving straight out made me seem suspicious. I knew that if anyone had asked about me coming and going, I could just come clean and tell them that I was homeless, but I still wanted to remain under the radar if I could. So, taking a bird bath at Kroger wasn't an everyday thing for me. Twice a week I would go, but I'd be careful to mix up the days.

My food temptation reminded me of when Steve Harvey was telling listeners about his past homeless situation on the radio. He lived in his car for years, while trying to excel in his career as a comedian. He would go into the store with a buggy, looking like a regular customer, then go to the bread and bologna aisle to get his items to make a delicious sandwich. He even was bold enough to dress it up the way he liked it. As he was explaining it, you can just imagine him strolling around taking a bite out of a sandwich that he had no intention of paying for. With a look on his face the whole time that was like, "Yeah, so what?" Like he didn't give a *damn!* Listening to how far he came since then gave me a small boost of energy to keep pressing on. I was bold, but not like Mr. Harvey, and besides, I kept a little money on me, but I wouldn't take my first bite to eat till lunch time or whenever the job was finished. That was how I maintained a low budget income. What had scared me the most about his situation is that he lived in his car for *years* before his life turned around for the better. It had only been a couple of months for me, and I was already falling apart.

CHAPTER 6
THROWING IN THE TILE

My monthly payments for my SUV were well overdue. The dealership had been calling all my references, trying to figure out where I was. They had no clue. My family kept texting and calling me to let me know they were looking for it, but I would just say okay and leave it at that. Nobody knew where I worked or where I was sleeping. It was all a well-kept secret. This was my "mobile" home they were trying to take from me… though, technically, it was theirs. But there was no way in hell I was going to hand over the keys without a fight. The winter season hadn't even started yet, and temperatures at night already weren't getting above 50 degrees. Being without a vehicle would mean that I would have to find some place to sleep outside, and a ride to work. Not going to happen. My thoughts were to keep it until the wheels fell off, or somehow save enough money to get another vehicle. If they did somehow find it, they would have to tow it away with me in it because I was not going to sleep under a bridge, at the park, or stay in a shelter.

When they called my phone, I would send it straight to voicemail. They used to call from the same number all the time, but then they started to switch numbers. If I didn't know the number, I would let it go to voicemail anyway. Sneaky little suckers.

It was getting ridiculous how late at night they would call. On one occasion, I did answer and told them that they can come and get it. When they asked for the address to pick it up, I gave them the University of Michigan's address. I knew my family had to have told them I was in Michigan, because after my own special tour that I did I sent Keisha pictures of the school. She didn't know how long I would be up there, or if that was my plan to stay. "You can try to come and get it, but good luck cause it's snowing up here," I said to the lady on the phone. They had their own tow truck service. The lady had asked me when I started to attend school there. I told her in the fall, which was the season we were currently in. At first, she was talking like they were going to take the trip, but then told me it sounded too good to be true. "Well, I told you everything, even where to pick it up at." The conversation ended. It would suck for them if they made that long trip only to come up empty handed. It was survival mode for me. Anything I could do or say to buy me more time, I would do or say. Then weeks went by with no more calls from unknown numbers. Maybe they had let it go? Well, at least they weren't calling my phone anymore.

Dealing with the stress and anxiety of trying to survive day-by-day was getting to me. I decided to inhale another drug that I was totally against. I tried weed before, but it had been long ago with a group of friends. But this time I'd have it all to myself and hopefully I would get so high it would put me in another realm of thought. That is the most common effect it had on people that I was aware of at the time. I knew where to get it, so my only problem was that I didn't know how to roll it up in a tight blunt. This is going to be an interesting challenge, I thought.

I made my purchase, then headed back to the parking lot. Looking at YouTube to learn how to roll a perfect blunt was out of the question. My old fashioned TracFone didn't have internet. After breaking down the weed, the hard part was next. Trying many times to get it rolled up where it would stay, I rolled it up the best I could—which was sloppy—and sparked it up. Bad news. All the weed fell out and I didn't even get a single pull off it. Shitttt! There are some things that I'm good at, and some things I'm not. Rolling a blunt was definitely something I needed more practice at.

As the days went on, it became harder and harder for me to keep fighting. My mind became fixated on when I would get out of this situation. Would I be homeless for one or two years, maybe longer? I tried to think positive by saying the ole phrase, "Whatever doesn't *kill* you makes you stronger." Well, this situation just might. Stress was building up, Ladonna was moving on to another relationship, and my family only called in to tell me that the dealership was looking for my SUV. I guess since I was *not* telling them that sleeping in my SUV was my new home, they assumed I was okay. But I wasn't. This was freaking hell to me! I didn't see them being much help either because they had their own family to raise. Mom would be a shoulder to lean on, but she wasn't present. Work and the blessing of having a vehicle were the only things that kept me from sleeping under a bridge. There was no other choice but to get up and go each morning. As I drive by and see homeless people today, I can't help but wonder what their stories are. Some might be more horrific and dramatic than mine, and others might be a lot more subtle, but they're all still stories that could have a positive effect on many people's lives. Letting other people know, that's going through a difficult time that they're not alone feels good.

If you had talked to me back then, I would seem normal. If you told a joke, I would laugh. If you asked how I was doing, I would say fine. But the truth was, I was in complete darkness. Didn't feel like talking, laughing, and I definitely wasn't fine. With all the drama and turmoil I was dealing with, I decided to punch out on the clock of life. I got a motel for the day. This was my own going away party, in room 212. I'd rented out that room before. It had powerful shower jets that felt like you were getting a massage. It had been days since my body was clean, and I wanted to treat myself.

Feeling thirsty for lust, I called Ladonna to see if she wanted to spend the night. Denied! One of the reasons that kept me around was that some days she would spend time with me, but of course that was only when she felt like it. If she had been present, there was no way I was going to commit such a horrible act. I wouldn't even think about ending my life.

After retrieving all the prescription pills I had left from my mom, I opened up the bag and emptied out all the bottles on the bed. I poured out the Oxycontin pills on the table. They were the money makers, but nobody could afford to come to me on a consistent basis due to the price of $20 a pill. I wouldn't pay that much for them, but that was the street value. There was also a bottle of morphine that had at least thirty pills in it. I poured them all out on the bed too, and just gazed at them for a bit. I had the most of them out of everything. *Is this what death looks like?* When I tried to see if I could grab all of them with one hand and couldn't, it made me realize that this was it. It was like Pez candy spread all over the bed. I glanced over at my large soda cup that I bought earlier, then back at the pills. Then I looked back at the cup. "Oh shit. I'm really about to do this." No one could save me at this point. It felt like it was a challenge to get them all down at once. It was scary and crazy at the same time.

My mind shifted to the Oxycontin. As I sat at the table in the room, I began to crush them up with my card, one by one. Just like the gangster movies had shown me. I took out a dollar bill and rolled it up to fit inside my nostril. With one finger closing a nostril, and the other open for business, the snorting took place. I did it over and over and over again, until the table was clean. Then it was time to put the icing on the cake. I made my way over to the bed. "Well… here goes all or nothing." Hand full by hand full, the morphine meds slithered down my throat. After chugging some drinks, I went another round. I got confirmation when there were no more pills left on the bed or table. That night, I took over twenty morphine pills alone. Then it was only a matter of time before I met my Creator.

The effects started off subtle, with just a slurring of my speech, then my vision became blurry. My lust for sex was long gone by then. I just needed a lady figure to comfort me. So, once again, I gave Ladonna a call. Like the moment before, denied! She would let me pick up my son, but she wasn't going to come to the room. Tre-Tre was only two years old at the time. With the effects kicking in the way that they were, I wasn't sure how much longer I would be able to take care of myself, let alone my child. She thought that I was smoking due to the slurring of my speech when she could barely understand me. The conversation ended with no luck of her showing up. I wasn't afraid of dying, I just wanted peace as most people would say when attempting suicide. After saying my prayers, I dozed off.

The next day, I woke up. That amazed me. I was sure there was no coming back. I wasn't relieved that I didn't die nor was I annoyed that I was still alive. I didn't know how to feel. It felt like I needed bifocals to navigate myself around. That's how bad my vision had gotten. It was in the afternoon when I finally got out of bed to use the bathroom, with my body slumped over because my stomach felt like it was in knots. I had discovered the weirdest thing. Though I had to go bad, the pee couldn't flow with me standing up. When I sat down, it could. I wasn't hungry, but knew I had to get a bite to eat of something. My appetite had faded away, along with my vision. At the motel office there was a soda machine. My mouth was dry, and that was the closest place to get a chilled drink. I sat and contemplated it for a bit. The distance seemed like a mile away from where I was because of my situation, but in reality, it was only a short walking distance. I braved up and started on my journey to walk up straight and normal, hoping no one would see me.

I reserved a room at the motel for two nights. I was trash. After downing some of my drink, I felt as if my body was feeling different than before. I laid back down on the bed and tried to go to sleep.

Well, if this is it then I need to pray one last time and text my family to let them know I have forgiven them. I thought about it… and couldn't build up enough courage to text everyone.

I didn't want to get hit with the question of why I hadn't forgiven them and myself for being angry with my family when standing in front of God. Everything else would have to flow out truthfully and sincerely, and I could only hope that I wouldn't get sentenced to life in hell. The only person I called was Keisha, and I knew she would spread the word about me forgiving them. After that, I was more than ready for whatever was going to happen to me. I found myself waking up the next day again at check out time. My vision was starting to get back to normal, and my stomach felt a little bit better, but I still couldn't stand while peeing. Didn't understand it. Even when I had to go bad and stood there for a moment, nothing came out, but as soon as I sat down, I started to pee. My stay ended without me taking a nice shower as I had intended on doing.

The last time I'd eaten anything was the day before. A fast-food restaurant was no doubt the only choice. Still not 100 percent okay, I walked in and ordered a burger and fries. My energy was completely gone. I could've fallen asleep in one of the lounge chairs in the lobby, if only there wasn't anyone else around.

.

CHAPTER 7
MISSING PIECE TO MY PUZZLE

It has been weeks now since the last time I felt a woman's touch. That was despite being very persistent with Ladonna about her spending some much needed time with me. She would talk to me on the phone, but not see me in person. Her and Mike were getting even closer. I tried with all my might to end their relationship as friends. Then there was one day when she was making up excuses for why she couldn't see me, but what she was saying wasn't making sense. I drove over to the house and looked through the living room window, where the blinds were open. My heart sank more than ever before. They both were there, on the couch. There was nothing I could do. I knew there would be a chance that she would be with him, but did not think they would be on the couch together like that. My body was filled with sad and angry emotions.

Everyone has felt that type of way before if they've ever been in love… that feeling you get when you catch your partner cheating or have an unexpected break-up. Me busting in her mom's house and kicking his ass is what I wanted to do, but it would not solve anything. With not much to say or do, I let them be and drove off.

A couple of days later, I contacted Slick and received another round of crack. I felt the same effects—loss of appetite and eyes buck wide open—and I drove back to Ms. Spank's house and walked straight in. Mike stood in the kitchen. Without no hesitation, I gave my opinion about him with my mouth right up to his ear so he could hear me clearly.

"I don't fucking like you."

"I did nothing wrong. I'm good, bruh."

"You need to leave," I said, standing right up close to him, ready to knock every one of his teeth out.

Ladonna ran upstairs to alert her mother of all the mayhem that was about to take place. They both rushed downstairs to stop it.

"Terrance, she told you she don't date anyone. She is single!"

"I don't care about that. I don't like him."

I knew he would be drunk around my child when I was not there. He was an alcoholic, and it was clear to see.

"I'm gone," he said.

"Terrance, you need to leave too," Ms. Spank said.

I was fine with that outcome, since he was leaving as well. Later that night, I showed back up to make sure my enemy had stayed clear. When I walked in the house unannounced, I saw Ladonna in the living room.

"Who is that just walking in my house?!" Ms. Spank yelled from upstairs.

"Terrance!" Ladonna said.

"Terrance, get the hell out my house!"

My body instantly gravitated to the sound of her voice coming from upstairs. I opened her bedroom door and there she was, sitting on her bed watching television.

"What is wrong with you Terrance?"

"I don't know."

"You do know. Look at you. Look at your eyes. Who did you get it from, Slick?"

"Yeah."

"You know your mother wouldn't be proud of you doing this if she were still alive."

"I'm just going through tough times right now."

"Don't you know you easily can be hooked on that."

"Psssshh, not me. I just did it to try it."

"Please get help Terrance. I don't want to see you throw your life away."

"That's not going to happen."

The conversation ended *without* me getting permission to stay the night, but Ladonna didn't care, so I stayed without Ms. Spank ever knowing. The next day, in the afternoon, Mike came knocking at the door. Ladonna and I had already been up. There we were, both under the same roof and both chasing after the same girl, but too manly to admit it. They both acted calm, like everything was normal. I stayed for a couple of hours before leaving with him still in the house. I got what I needed the night before to relieve built up tension and stress. All was good on my end.

Christmas of 2012 was a good time. I didn't know how I was going to plan it, but I wanted my son to stay with me the first half of Christmas Day. The other half he could spend with his mother, as stated in the court papers. The motel room that I chose fit my budget. It was needed for me to have a successful holiday with my son. I left the presents in the trunk of my car. When he fell asleep, it was time to play Santa Claus… the version of him that delivered to motels. I put the presents in the corner, all stacked up. I was proud of myself for still being able to give my son Christmas presents despite my situation.

The morning came, and I woke him up so he could see all the presents he had. It really was like three or four presents stacked on top of each other to make it seem like it was a lot. To him, he could not tell the difference being that he was only two years old. Any amount of presents for a kid that young is always an exciting time. With a big smile on his face, he rushed out of bed to open them up. I had bought myself some new clothes a few weeks earlier and was saving them to wear on that day. I had been saving up money from work and donating plasma to make it all happen. This might be my last Christmas, so I wanted to look nice and treat myself to an outfit and shoes. We both got dressed and headed to Ms. Spank's house.

Instead of being greeted with warm smiles and a Merry Christmas, we walked into yelling and screaming. Family members arguing on Christmas Day. I did not understand it, but I stayed for a little bit, with Mike still there sitting in the kitchen while I was in the living room. I didn't want to go back to the motel and be alone on a big important holiday. After an hour of what seemed like a drama TV show, I decided to go to Tracy's house to see what she was doing.

Her sister let me in and went upstairs to tell Tracy I was there. She came downstairs. With just me and her in the living room we conversated for a bit. She seemed pretty relaxed as she held her newborn in her hands while we talked about casual things. Even though I looked nice, I still didn't have the courage to ask her out. She was a package deal. I couldn't just have her all to myself, it would be her plus her two sons. I daydreamed about moving in with her, but knew that was a long shot. Even if I did move in, trouble was right down the street. As the day ended, reality set back in. The next day came, and just when I thought my life couldn't get any worse… it did.

I drove over to Ms. Spank's house to visit Ladonna. She was not there, so I decided to wait. Demetrius, her brother, wanted to get a game but needed a ride. Who better else to ask than me. His mother didn't have a car. In my mindset, if there is money to be made, I'm going to get it. Every dime counts.

"Hey man, I need a ride to the game store."

"I gotcha. You got $20 for gas?"

"Naw. I just got enough to get a game."

"I can't take you then."

"What about if I give you $5?"

"*Hahaha*! $5 will get you dropped off down the street."

"C'mon man."

"It's got to be twenty. My SUV is a gas guzzler, and the game store is *not* a short drive."

"Fuck you and your vehicle!" he yelled.

At that moment, I knew it was serious.

"Okay. Ride the bus then."

"Fuck you!"

"I hear you talking, but ain't doing nothing."

He quickly approached me as I was sitting down. I rose, thinking he was about to swing. The argument grew louder and louder. I mugged him with my hand.

"Get outta my face!" I said.

Ms. Spank rushed downstairs to see what the commotion was all about.

"Momma, he just put his hands on me! He mugged me!"

"I sure did! You shouldn't have been in my face!"

"Y'all just calm down. What's going on here?"

"He just mad cause I wouldn't take him to buy a game."

He was in the background yelling, trying to get through to his mom that I had put my hands on him.

"He just mugged me! He just mugged me! Fuck it, I'm ready to fight now!"

"No! Y'all are not about to fight in here!"

He spoke with confidence, "We can take it outside then!"

"Whatever you want to do, it don't matter," I said.

"Yeah, y'all take that mess outside."

I never back down from a fight, doesn't matter how big or small the person is. At the end of the day, if I did lose, at least he didn't run me home. If it were a group of people wanting to jump me, then that would be a different story. I had been jumped before, back when I was a kid and thought that I was untouchable and could take them all… but I was wrong. I've learned from my past, and now know not to let my ego get my ass kicked by a group of guys. This situation was going to be a one-on-one. At least that's what I thought.

Once we both were outside, with his mom looking on, there was no more talking. He threw the first punch. I countered with a straight jab. Right when I was about to body slam him on the ground, someone snatched my shirt and started nailing me on the back of the head. I felt every blow. *This is supposed to be a one-on-one fight. Why is she jumping in*? I tried my best to continue to focus on him, but the blows kept coming, and they were heavy. "Get off my brother!" she yelled. That's when I realized it wasn't his mom, but his older sister. His mom was still watching. His sister had been upstairs the whole time and had run out right in the middle of the fight.

We were fighting until one of us stopped. I'm no quitter, so the fight must continue until he tapped out, or his sister knocked me out from the solid blows she was throwing to the back of my skull. I tried pushing her away from me, but when I did, her brother would come in and try to land some licks. He got one good lick in by kneeing me in the nuts. The mayhem ended when he couldn't see any more out of his eye that was covered in a sea of blood. My adrenaline was pumping so much that I didn't realize it had gotten to that point. That was the end of it. He kept talking smack, but for me, my job was done. There was no need to argue back. I walked away. Ms. Spank called him in the house, and we went our separate ways. When I got in my vehicle to drive off, that's when I started feeling the pain coming from my nuts. *"Damn, this hurts so bad!"* After that I needed somewhere to hang out to make the day go by faster. When I pulled up to Tracy's house the next day, she let me in. Her two sisters and her were sitting in the living room.

"What up my people," I said.

"I heard about you," Tracy said.

"What about me?"

"You were fighting with Demetrius."

"Aw, that was nothing. Ms. Spank banned me from her house, this will be my next chill spot," saying it in a joking manner, but serious at the same time.

Tracy didn't believe me that I was banned from Ms. Spank home until her sister confirmed it. Tracy and I conversated over that topic for a short while, but there was no bragging coming from my end. She was in the middle of cooking, so I came up with a deal that if I bought some juice that go with the meal, she would invite me to dinner. She grinned, but never gave me a yes or no answer. Without a definite answer meant, to me, that she didn't care. I got the drinks as promised and everything went well. The steaks she made with the sides were amazing. I must have gotten too relaxed when I was upstairs with her son playing the game, when all of a sudden I heard,

"Terrance, it's time for you to go. We about to get ready for bed."

"I'm spending the night."

"No you not!"

I had brushed it off because I wanted to sleep somewhere other than my SUV or a motel for once. A couple of minutes passed. She yelled again from downstairs,

"Terrance, it's time for you to go!"

There was no negotiating at this point. She wanted me gone. So back to the back seat of my vehicle I went.

Most of the time when I called her, she would pick up or call me back. Now that I was in good with her, it was time for me to ask her an important question. I called my future boo up. The conversation started off by talking about random things like we always did. It was driving me crazy, wanting to ask her but not having the courage to do it. It was time to get straight to the point,

"I been liking you, and I know you like me, so why don't we become a couple?"

"*Hahahahahaha!*"

"What?! You laughing, but I'm serious."

"I don't want Ladonna to come up here banging on my door starting something she can't finish."

"Why are you worried about her?"

"I'm not worried. It's just a lot of drama that I don't want to be a part of."

"I got you. You don't have to worry about that."

"No."

"Mannnn bye," and I hung up.

My heart was crushed. We had good conversations, and there never was a problem when I was going over to her house to chill. It was hard for me to come back to myself after that rejection, but I clearly understood why. It sucks thinking she was the missing piece to my puzzle, and it all backfired on me. What else could I do, besides keep trying and bugging her day-after-day by flirting and letting her know

I only wanted to be with her? With some women, that might work, so I gave it a shot. Each time that I flirted, or asked her out I got a, nope, no, or never in response. Always.

I was lonely, and needed someone in my corner to keep me company. After the first rejection, I knew my destiny to be with her was over, but I kept trying to prove myself wrong. While sitting on Tracy's porch, she shared with me a rumor that was going around.

"I need to talk to you," she said.

"About what?"

"Ms. Spank told me you and your baby momma got a motel room, which I don't care about that, but now Ladonna be looking at me funny and enough is enough, so you can't come back over here no more."

"Why you listening to her in the first place?"

"I'm not. Just don't come back."

"It's like that for real?"

"Yeah."

"Okay."

And that was the end of that. Ms. Spank knew I was chilling at Tracy's place, but this was a way to pay me back for beating up her son. Oh well, life goes on.

CHAPTER 8
DEAD END

Ladonna wasn't upset about the fight between me and her brother. We talked about it, and it became clear that I was only defending myself. I was boring to her. That's why she cut off our friendship. The people that I called my friends were never around. And when they were outside, it was just to hang out on the block. I needed female companionship. Someone I could get close with. Nobody ever knew the truth of my situation. Not Tracy, not Ladonna, not my friends, not even family members. Even to this day, my family don't know what I went through being homeless. I've told them bits and pieces, but when they get ahold of this book, only then they will finally know the whole truth about my experience of feeling like I was alone in complete darkness. It was a big secret hanging over my head, but I had control over it.

If I gave it time, Ladonna would pop back into my life like she always did. But when? That was the big question. She was the only one that I could potentially hold at night to let go of some stress. I knew that would come with some of its own stress and drama, but I obviously didn't care enough to let her go fully.

Days went by without speaking to anyone. Satan had all the equipment to use my thoughts as his playground. While sitting in my vehicle, I glanced over and saw some paper and a pencil. I was going to start writing my day-to-day events down, but something else came to mind. Without hesitation, the pencil began to move.

Die kill yourself die
Die kill yourself die
Die kill yourself die

Why would I fall in despair and write something like that repeatedly, like it was write-offs? It seemed like boredom became my best friend. Everything that used to bring me joy, laughter, and love, was gone for good. Some people that were behind bars seemed to be better off than me, and I'm the one supposed to be feeling free. But free how? My mind, that once was limitless, was trapped in a little box and labeled with two words, give up. With that notice, I surrendered.

My life shouldn't be this difficult. Why does it feel like everyone is turning their backs on me? How long will I be in this situation? Why can't I even be a real father to my son? God is putting me through the trenches. How long can I keep a straight face and act like everything is okay when it isn't? I thought.

I was still going through the motions by showing up for work and donating plasma so I could stay above water. All of that was growing old though. My life was stuck. It didn't matter how hard I tried to get ahead, it always seemed like it was never enough. It been weeks since I last saw Ladonna, which meant no sex. At least sex would take away some stress that I was dealing with. It would take a miracle for that to happen again though. I called her up on New Year's Eve to see if she was going to celebrate bringing in the big day with me. After begging her, she finally agreed and told me to call her back. Night came, and around 10 o'clock I gave her a call. Her mom picked up and told me she wasn't at home. No need to stress. There's still time. At least her mom would deliver the message to her that I called, and hopefully she would call me back. 11pm came around, still no call. Around 11:30 was when I called again,

"Hello."

"Put Ladonna on the phone."

"Hold on."

It was Mike that answered. I didn't stress over it. It was obvious they were messing around, so I kept my cool. He claimed he had just walked in the house when I called. From what I was told from Ladonna weeks ago, Ms. Spank had given him a key and he was now living with them.

"She upstairs asleep bruh."

"Go wake her up. It is something important I need to tell her."

"Okay."

He came back to the phone minutes later.

"She's not getting up."

"All right." *Click.*

There was a bottle of sleeping pills within my reach, and I had swallowed all of them. *"I'm tapping out."* I got in my sleeping position and dozed off. It was January 1, 2013, when I found myself waking up around 12:30am, hoping that I had a missed call from her. Nothing. Waking up that soon after taking a whole bottle of sleeping pills meant God was still looking out for me. I got comfortable and dozed off again.

I waited until the afternoon rolled around when I knew she would be up. I was expecting her to call before I made the first move. It didn't happen. My time came to call her again. She answered,

"Hello."

"I thought you were going to bring in the new year with me yesterday. What happened?"

"Me and my sister went downtown. I forgot to call you, and plus, I was too tired."

"Well… you still want to hang out?"

"No. I think it would be better if we just talk on the phone."

"What about later on?"

"No!"

"*Damnnnnn.* it's like that?"

"Terrance, I'm busy, bye. *Click*!"

I found a knife in my vehicle. I didn't know where it came from, or how it got in there, but I grabbed it and thought for a moment. The time had come for me to follow through with what had been on my mind. *Since the pills didn't do the job, this will.* I took it to my arm and sliced it. It left a scratch on the first stroke. I applied even more pressure on the second one. A little trickle of blood came out, but it wasn't good enough. I called Ladonna back.

"What Terrance?!"

"Please, can we talk?"

"I told you. If you want to talk to me, it will be on the phone."

"But I have to tell you something, and it need to be face-to-face."

"Whatever you have to tell me, you can tell me on the phone. I am *not* meeting up with you." *Click!*

This time I hung up in her face. I placed my arm by the door, because the next cut would cause a lot of blood to pour out. To most people, it was New Year's Day. For me, I called it Doomsday. I held the knife against my wrist and applied pressure to it as I slowly moved the blade across. "Fuck! This hurts!" I knew the key for less pain was to do it fast, and so I did. I made a papercut size slice. I could do better than that, I thought I gritted my teeth and gave it my all. *Whoosh*! "Aweeeeee! Fuuuuuuck!" In my head, it had to be completed. There was no other way to deal with all of the shit going on. There was nothing left to do but to express my emotions freely. Anger, pain, sorrow, and darkness they all descended and surrounded and embraced me like they were my close friends. I cried, every tear releasing the pressure I was holding back by trying to pretend like everything was cool all along. I decided to give Ladonna another call. At that point, praying wasn't an option. I needed to talk to someone, and soon. Crying in front of a lady makes me feel uncomfortable. I got my emotions under control before dialing her number.

"Hello."

"Please, can we meet up? It will be quick."

"Okay, but you can't park in front of the house cause my mom don't want you nowhere near here."

I parked my vehicle a block away from where she lived, then called her back up to let her know I was at the spot. She came out and hopped in.

"What is it?"

"I can't go on with life no more. I feel like dying." Tears flowed freely from my eyes as I kept explaining. "Look, I already tried once to kill myself," I showed her the cuts. The truth of the matter was, I'd tried to commit suicide many times before that. The cuts on my wrist were just the visible scars.

"What the fuck Terrance!"

"I'm tired of struggling and dealing with life. I want it to end. My body feels heavy. I don't even want to move."

"Terrance, you are depressed."

"Naw, it's not that."

"Yes, you are. Trust me. When I was depressed, the only thing that I did was lay in bed all day."

She was explaining exactly how I was feeling. As I gazed out the front window, my dark side was still inside of me and it didn't want to come clean about what was really going on. That story I had already given her about living with my uncle was good enough for her to think it was the reason I was having such a tough time dealing with life.

"You need to go to the hospital. You want me to go with you?"

“Yeah,” I said, as I wiped away my tears, “but don’t tell anybody about this.”

“I won’t. Let me get some shoes.”

She gave me a hug and left. My heart felt warm again, knowing there was someone out there who still cared. I thanked God for that confirmation that He was still on the throne, watching over me. Moments later, she hopped back in and we went to the hospital. Our ride there was silent. Not even music coming from the radio. There was so much that needed to be said, but for the life of me, it would not come out.

To this day, she still doesn’t know the full truth. She won’t know until she picks up this book and reads it. I still can’t explain why it’s so hard for me to share that side of my story with her. It must be something along the lines of trust issues.

At the hospital, she did most of the talking. I didn’t have the courage to tell them about my suicidal thoughts and actions just for them to look at me all crazy. But there was no strange behavior, which made me feel more comfortable. After talking with the clerk at the front desk, it was time for us to sit and wait for a doctor to see me. I glanced around and saw the room was half full. *Great*, I thought, it was going to take a long time. Then the assistant came out.

“Terrance? Terrance McAdoo?”

Me and Ladonna looked at each other. “That was quick,” we both said.

It hadn’t even been fifteen minutes. The nurse led us to the other wing of the hospital. Nobody was there, not even staff members.

“You can take this room right here and a doctor will be with you shortly,” the nurse said before leaving us alone.

“Is this the place where they take all the crazy people?”

“Hahaha I guess so… you the only one that’s back here,” Ladonna said.

I grinned, “You got jokes now.”

We both sat on the couch. I laid my head on her chest while trying to get the stains off her coat until a doctor came for me.

"Where did these stains come from?"

"On New Year's Eve, me and my sister partied downtown. On our way back, I bought an ice cream but spilled it all over myself. When she dropped me off at home, I crashed. That's why I didn't call you."

We waited and waited. Finally, a nurse came and told me they were transporting me to a Crisis Stabilization Unit (C.S.U). That was my only option to get better. There wasn't anything for me on the outside, and on top of that it was a place where I could actually sleep in a bed. My SUV stayed in the garage at the hospital during my stay.

"You must tell your friend to leave now. Sorry," the nurse said.

She called her sister to pick her up. We hugged each other and said our goodbyes. She got up and proceeded to the door.

"Love you," I said, hoping she would say it back. There was no response.

She left the room. It hurt a little, but her presence still comforted me even when she wasn't in the room. Moments later, she came back.

"Okay, I'm leaving now."

"I love you."

"I love you too. Call me," she said.

"Stay by the phone. I will call as soon as I get to CSU."

"Okay."

That was confirmation that she was going to stand by her word. There was still a soft spot in her heart for me. Not long after that, I was transported to CSU I was picturing that would mean padded rooms and people with severe mental issues screaming all night… none of that was present. After the lady gave me a tour of the place, I called Ladonna and her mom answered the phone,

"Hello."

"Can I speak to Ladonna?"

"She's not here. Who is this?"

"This is Terrance."

"Oh hey, she went somewhere with her sister."

"Do you know when she will be back?"

"Naw."

"You taking care of yourself?"

"Yes. Tell her to call me when she gets in."

"Okay."

My heart was crushed. Ladonna had given me her word that she would answer when I called, but she was nowhere to be found.

That phone call left me feeling deep disappointment. I went to the break room to watch TV for a little bit before it was lights out. I was hungry, but there was nothing to eat but some saltine crackers that were being passed around.

"Is this what y'all have for snacks?" I said to one of the guys.

"Yup. The food is put up for today."

I walked over to the coffee station. I don't like coffee, but I just had to try and satisfy my stomach with something. I poured a lot of cream and sugar in it to hide the grimy taste of the coffee beans. The first cup I drank was a tough one to get down. After two sips of the second cup, that was it for me. I hoped it would be enough to take my mind off being hungry until breakfast the next day.

"Everyone go to your rooms. It's time for bed," the clerk said.

I tried one more time to call and see if she would pick up. She didn't. It hurt. I'd trusted her, and ended up being disappointed. After repeatedly going through the same thing, one would think that's enough. But I'm persistent. Each time it hurts just as if it was the first. I can't seem to get rid of the revolving cycle.

I had a room to myself, but there were two beds, as well as a sink and a shower. The employees would wash your clothes if you needed them to. I fought off my sleep thinking she would return my call, but that never happened. Moments later, I dozed off only to wake up to a nurse who was trying to check my temperature and blood pressure. Soon after she finished, I went back to sleep.

The next day, I woke up to a roommate. Everybody had to get up at the same time to have our breakfast and conversation. I didn't want to speak to him about the reason why he was there. I didn't know what might come out his mouth. "Good morning," he said. I responded just to be polite. And behold, he told me the one thing I *didn't* want to hear. Suicidal thoughts were common in this place, but his reason for being admitted left me feeling uncomfortable. He heard *voices* in his head that controlled his movements. What if one of those mindless people told him to kill me while I was resting in my bed?! He seemed cool for the moment, but I was still on guard at all times.

"There is no way of blocking them out. No matter how hard I try," he said.

That was scary to me. I mean, if I was going to hurt someone, it would be myself… not someone else because some fictional being told me to. I got up to take a shower and met everyone in the break room. There was a long table that seated us all.

The food that they served for breakfast was a ridiculously small portion. There wasn't any bacon, eggs, sausages, or even leftovers. We all received a small amount of hash browns. I was hoping for a continental style breakfast, and couldn't remember the last time I had one.

"Y'all feeding us like we on a diet," one guy said.

"I know, but this is all we can give. It's part of our guidelines," the lady said.

There was no one in there that was overweight. The biggest guy seemed like he weighed about 200 pounds, but it fit him. I thought the food would be amazing, but was yet again disappointed.

"We still got lunch to look forward to, so maybe they will make up for it," I said.

After we ate our "diet" meal, it was time for storytelling. Each of us had to tell the group the reason we were there.

I remember one guy's story more than anyone else's. He appeared to be in his late 20s. When it was his turn to talk, he froze. We could all tell this one would hit home as he chewed on his bottom lip, trying not to make eye contact with anyone. The room fell silent. We waited patiently, giving him time to gather his thoughts.

"Umm… umm."

Then there was silence again. All eyes were on him as he struggled to pull the words out of his mouth. I thought the lady that led the group would pass him and come back when he was ready to talk, but she sat there waiting for him to spit it out.

"Umm."

I was thinking she could see that he was having a difficult time, and was wondering why she wasn't giving him some time to gain control of his emotions. That never happened. He sat there, staring at the table, for what seemed like a full two minutes. You could hear a pen drop. Then words left his mouth while he stared at the table.

"I'm here because… my son died."

He was fighting hard not to break down crying.

"He was riding… with my girlfriend, when they were involved in a car… accident."

Tears started to flow down his cheeks, dripping onto the table.

"Now I can't get him ready for school in the mornings, which I loved doing. Both are dead! So there's no reason for me to live anymore."

This was fresh. I can't remember if he was having thoughts of ending his life, or if he'd made an attempt, but that outcome was touchy for everyone. The guy sitting adjacent to him started to ball out tears himself.

"We all have a horrifying story to tell. B-b-but that is really something. I'm sorry to hear that brother." He tried to control the flow of his tears by wiping them off, but more came to replace them. *"I'm here for you man... we all are."* Everyone in the room gave their confirmation.

"Yeah."

"Yup."

"I'm here too."

"I will be praying for you."

That's when the guy that told us the story let his tears flow freely. The group leader told him he needed to get some *serious* counseling, and she would help him set it up. He nodded and got up to get some tissues.

That was a deal breaker for everyone. None of our stories were that bad. To lose his *son,* and his *girlfriend, a*t the *same time* on the *same day…* how does someone come back from that? That's a sad story, but maybe one we all needed to hear. His situation was at the top of the peak compared to ours. When you think your situation is bad, there always will be someone that is going through a lot more.

They had a big book full of random numbers for different housing facilities like homeless shelters, half-way housing, rehab centers, etc. Most of the numbers were old and not in service. Each number I dialed was a dead end.

I called Keisha to give her an update on my situation. I told her about me getting high, and where I was staying, but never about my attempt to saw off my wrist. She gave me words of encouragement.

After spending my two days max in CSU, it was time for me to head back to the streets by default. I spoke with the clerk in the hallway alone.

"It's time for me to go."

"Okay, which facility we need to transport you to?"

"I'm going back to my vehicle."

"What?! You don't want to do that… and besides, it's getting colder by the day out there. Have you tried calling all the numbers in that book?" she said, pointing to it.

"Yeah, most of them are a no-go."

"Well, the best we can do is offer you one more day, but it will be in one of the rooms in the back."

The room she was referring to was what came to mind when I first heard about that place. A padded room. I politely answered, "Naw, I'm cool."

Living in my SUV was better than staying there. Yeah, it was nice and warm, and there was an actual bed to lay in, with a sink and toilet, but they fed you only to leave you hungry for more. When you start to get settled in, it's time to go. I'd made up my mind and wasn't going to change it back.

"Well okay. Good luck."

"Thanks."

They gave me a survey to fill out at the end of my stay to help them provide a better service. At the end of the page was a space to add a comment. I wrote, need to provide larger portions of food and extend the stay.

It was two days maximum, I understood that, and the place wasn't that big and there were plenty of other people that needed help that meant they couldn't take care of them all at once. I gathered up my things, said goodbye to my roommate, and waited on the transport van in the lobby to take me back where I left my vehicle.

It was afternoon by the time I was reunited with my "mobile home." That whole ordeal was an experience, and a chapter that will go in my history book of places that I've traveled to. Not exactly my ideal destination, but it had significant meaning. The only thing on my mind at that moment was eating something big and juicy. I still had a couple of dollars left over from the temp service, so I went to a burger joint and ordered the biggest burger they had, and a large fry and drink. I ate in the restaurant while reminiscing on CSU.

After satisfying my stomach, it was time to go back to my old ways. Back to being bored, sitting in my vehicle at some random spot and waiting for nightfall. I told myself, "That was crazy! Wonder what life will throw at me next? Will I be able to handle it all? Can't be worse than what I've already faced."

CHAPTER 9
NEED RELAXATION.

At work, nobody knew where I had been. Neither did they bother asking. That was a good thing though because I wouldn't tell them if they did. It was common for people to disappear like I had and come back later.

That night, I took a shot in the dark to ask Michelle if I could just sleep at her place for a week. I thought the answer would be no. She knew there was a possibility that I'd mess with Ladonna, and was afraid that the unnecessary drama might come to her doorstep. But it's only for a week… surely she'd say yes. I went over to her place to ask. I didn't come out with it right away though. I started talking about random things. I was still afraid of being rejected. As she proceeded to go back to her room, the time was now or never.

"Can I stay with you for a week, so I can get back on my feet?"

I knew it would take a lot longer than a week, but it was for comfort and to save some money. With no hesitation, the answer was no. I didn't bother to ask why, but since it was dark out I figured she would let me stay the night, and I planned on being out by the next evening.

"You can spend the night, but early tomorrow morning is when you will have to leave."

"Okay."

I thought about it as I laid on her couch. My body was exhausted. I had planned to sleep in until at least eleven o'clock the next day, and not to be woken up any time sooner.

"It's alright. I'm about to head out."

We said our goodbyes, and that was it. It hurt that I could not sleep in, but I had to wear my poker face and head back to my vehicle like everything was fine.

I found another abandoned spot for that night to sleep. I was going wherever the wind blew. It seemed like I'd become numb to this whole life thing. My body was completely drained of energy. The freezing temperature outside wouldn't allow me to get warm, even with my clothes on and covers wrapped tightly around me. I couldn't take it anymore. My feet felt like bricks of ice. "There got to be a warm building somewhere that I can go to and sleep for a couple of hours." Instantly, the post office came to mind. The main lobby was closed, but where the P.O boxes were wasn't. I pulled up, and no cars were parked. It was after midnight, so that gave me assurance that no one would come by to get their mail. On the other hand, there still was a chance someone would pop up and see me laying on the floor, sleeping. thinking Me*, if someone catches me here, then I will leave. The worst thing that could happen is I get told to leave.* Since I fit the criteria of a homeless person, my situation of sleeping at the post office would be no different.

I looked around to see if there were any cameras, which there were, so I picked a hidden spot. I wasn't there to break into anybody's mailbox, or vandalize the property, it was strictly to catch up on much-needed sleep and stay warm. That was all. I got comfortable only to find myself tossing and turning out of fear that somebody might walk in and call the police, when there was no harm done. Then I'd have a much bigger situation on my hands. The cops would let me go with a warning not to show back up, or maybe they would just take me to jail for trespassing, I thought. My mind needed to be focused on getting some rest, and not dwelling on what could happen. I took my chances and tried not to think about the potential consequences. Then I heard some noise in the back, where they sort out the mail. Maybe my mind was playing tricks on me, but the same noise kept appearing. It was starting to get so stressful that I couldn't fall asleep with all these thoughts tumbling through my head. *Fuck it. I'm going back to the vehicle*. McDonalds was right across the street. I assumed they were about to open, so I decided to go there and wait with the other customers. We waited an hour before they unlocked the doors. I'd never have thought people would wait that long in the parking lot for a McDonalds to open. Once in, I went straight to the dollar menu and got me a little bite to eat, then sat in the lounge chair

NEED RELAXATION.

and took a cat nap. *Ahhhh. This feels good.*

Hours quickly flew by, and I knew it was time for me to switch locations. Didn't want people to know that I was using McDonald's for a place to sleep. Across the street from them was Burger King. I walked in as a customer, but it was to cover up what I really was there for. If I had walked in and gone straight to the dining area to sleep, they would have kicked me out on the spot. I strategically planned all of this out before it was time to execute. To my luck, it worked. But trouble stared me down behind the counter while I was eating my small meal. I knew him, and he knew me. Right when I took off my shoes to relax is when I spotted him.

Have you ever had that moment where you come in the house from a long day of work, and the only thing you want to do is relax? No talking on the phone, no texting friends, no checking emails, not even playing with your kids. Just pure relaxation. But right when you get relaxed you hear, "Mommmmmm! He's hurting me!" and your attention is needed elsewhere. That was that feeling. I thing first The was thought *damn, I'm about to fight again.* The cat nap that I had taken earlier was nothing. My body was still drained of energy. If it ever came to throwing punches, which I was for certain it would if he approached me, then I would give him all the sixtyv seconds my exhausted body would allow. After that, my only hope would be the fight getting broken up by bystanders. I went back to minding my own business, but every time I looked up his eyes were glued to me. That was confirmation. It was about to go down. I put my shoes back on to get ready for the inevitable showdown, because I wasn't about to leave. There was no other public place that I felt comfortable enough to rest in, and my SUV was out of the question. Whatever was going to happen, would happen. I wasn't going to budge.

He came out from behind the counter. In my peripheral vision, I could see him walking up. It wasn't until he got five feet from me when he started to talk,

"What's up mane?"

"Nothing just chilling."

"You remember me?"

"You Demetrius cousin, right?"

NEED RELAXATION.

"Yeah, I just want to hear your side of the story."

"My intentions weren't focused on fighting him, but he kept popping off at the mouth, so I handled my business."

"I told him once before he needed to watch his temper."

The way he was speaking to me didn't come off as threatening, but I was still on guard in case he tried to sneak in a punch.

"That's my cousin, and I had to put him in his place for running off at the mouth too. He lifts all them weights, and it's pointless if he can't fight. Where we live, people not afraid of nothing. He would have to prove to me he can back up what he says."

"I'm wit cha. He needs to put down them weights and pick up some boxing gloves."

"I didn't come over here to start a fight. I was curious on what happened."

"Okay, cool."

We gave each other daps, and he went back to work. Shortly thereafter, I was down and out with my head on the table and feet propped up on another chair.

It was still morning, so there weren't many people occupying the dining area which made me feel even more relaxed resting there. I was in there for hours without anyone disturbing me. When I finally woke up, it was after twelve in the afternoon. Temptation was begging me to stay there all day. Even though I didn't have anything else to do, I didn't want to overstay my welcome.

Across the room, there was another guy that was sleeping. Looked to be around my age. Thoughts ran through my mind about him possibly being homeless as well. He wasn't there when I got there. I sat up, preparing to finish what little bit of food that I'd left uneaten prior to dozing off. It had gotten cold and tasted nasty. I wasn't that hungry anyway, so I threw it in the trash. Sounds crazy, I know, being in my predicament and throwing away food like that when I was barely getting by, but I know many can relate.

For instance, if you get fresh fries from a fast-food restaurant and you let them get cold, there is no bringing back the freshness by heating them up in the microwave. They are done. There are just some foods out there that you will die of starvation before ever trying to revive. This was one of those cases. Trying to eat cold food that is supposed to be warm, when it's already freezing outside, will make you lose your appetite. I knew it would be a long while before I had my next meal, but my body had already adjusted to skipping meals throughout the day.

After throwing my meal away, I went to the restroom. Congratulations to me, Burger King was my new spot for a quick wash-up if I was in the area. The restroom was super big, and as an added bonus it came with a drain and a door you could lock. I could now get a nice, deep clean everywhere and not worry about flooding the restroom, which was right by the front door. I could wash up every day without the threat of being seen by the workers. As you can tell by now, I tried my best to stay under the radar as much as possible to limit the questioning of my presence wherever I went.

I thought long and hard about being a trashman. Went over the positives and negatives with myself. The positives? I'd get to work Monday through Friday. It would seem like a regular workday, with a steady weekly check. The negative side of it was having to get there around six in the morning and being exposed to the weather outside. It was cold in the mornings, and would especially be colder riding on the back of the trash truck. And the last downside—that I thought was the absolute worst, but which later proved to be something different—was the odor. After giving it some thought, I decided to lace up my boots and try it out.

Most neighborhoods we went to were middle class. Their trash bags were tightly sealed and organized. We could pick them up and throw them in the back, without the foul odor clinging to our clothes, but you will still get dirty. That part is inevitable. I was okay with it. I gave myself only a week to try it out. I didn't want to do it really, but it still was the experience I was gaining. After getting the experience, I figured this was all right. Only thing that was hard about it was getting there at six in the morning. Anything else was a breeze as we cruised along the city streets. As a kid, I always wanted to feel the thrill of riding on the back of the truck, and now I could live out one of my fantasies.

NEED RELAXATION.

In the mornings, it sucked. The winds hit so hard it felt like being choked while riding down the road, but in the afternoons, I enjoyed every bit of it. There was a lot of walking too, since not every house we caught a ride to. To me, walking was the least of my worries coming from an athletic background. I was starting to build up steam. There was steady income pouring in, and it felt like this was going to be my permanent position.

When we rode through rich neighborhoods, the residents would leave tips in envelopes on the trash can lids for us when we picked up their trash. The envelopes would be taped on there, or have an object holding them down. As we were approaching this one trash can, I saw a white paper. My eyes grew bigger as we approached. I hopped off the back, hoping it was what I thought. As I walked closer to it, within arm's reach, I heard the driver say,

"Hand me that envelope right there."

I thought whoever reached the tip first got to claim it... *nope!* That is not how they do things apparently. I handed it to him and was confused, but he explained,

"If y'all see an envelope on the lid, hand it to me. At the end of the day, I will split the money evenly."

"Yeah, that's straight," my partner said.

"Out of everybody that works for Labor Forcer, y'all two are the hardest workers."

I never tried to aim for that title. All I was doing was keeping my head above water while fighting my way, desperately trying to swim through life. Being labeled, "hardest workers" was a bonus. At the end of the workday, the driver kept his promise and split the money three ways. "I can get used to this," I said.

CHAPTER 10
MIXED EMOTIONS

Months had passed, and I'd survived the winter blues. It was now spring. There had to be somewhere that would accept me other than the shelter, I thought. I prayed that God would bless me with a spot to live in the country. Everything that I was going through was taking its toll. I needed a fresh start. I figured that going to the country and learning everything over again in a new environment with new faces would erase the negative thoughts that I was buried in. But also, I couldn't help but think of the worst when it came to living in the country as a Black person. I thought the majority of people in the country were racist, so it had to be in an area where it was isolated from society.

Even though I fit the requirements of a homeless person, I felt as if I was better off in my SUV than staying at the shelter. Living in a shelter comes with a curfew, I just couldn't see myself living there. A curfew would only hold me back from prospering because some work started at night or lasted until nightfall. An addition to that, the beds are limited. First come first serve bases. And besides, there were people that needed it more than me. At least my SUV had enough room to lie down in, and I could travel anywhere at any time.

I'm incredibly grateful that I was given so much freedom with it, but that got old. The feeling of walking into my *own* crib, with a *bed,* that would be real freedom. A place where I could take a long, hot shower and feel the water massaging my back. That was the new freedom I was searching for.

Getting a five-star, luxury apartment would be far-fetched for me… even though that crossed my mind plenty of times. Really any place I could call my own would suffice. I started applying for housing. One place seemed great, but the rejection left me devastated.

The next suitable place to live on my list was the projects. It's a rough community, but it was the only option I felt that I would get in with no problem. My intuition told me there were better options though, so I dug in and did my research on places that would accept someone like me. My only source of income, that could provide a pay stub, was Labor Forcer. Not the best, but at least it was something. By me showing proof of work, they would know I'm out here trying my best.

The library was my friend. It was where I went for entertainment, when I wasn't entertaining myself by fantasizing about hitting the lottery jackpot. The places I would travel, the houses and cars I would buy, the people I would socialize with, the things I would do to give back to communities living in poverty, that was my version of a perfect lifestyle. The library also was another place where I would pass the time.

While I was there one day, I pulled up a search on apartments that I could get. Some already came with cable hookups installed. All my listings were income based. My main goal was to get out of my SUV, and into something livable. I stopped applying after filling out a few applications. There was a waiting period of a couple of weeks to a month to see if you'd get approved. If I filled out all the applications, and every one of them got rejected, that would send me into a rage. I figured that by just filling out a few at a time, at least then the rejection blow would not be so harsh. If there were any.

In the meantime, I started looking for a permanent job in my career field as an electrician. I had already obtained the education and experience. There weren't a lot of companies hiring for that position. Over the winter, jobs had slowed down for most companies. That was usual. But now that it was Spring, I looked forward to the electrical companies being able to start hiring people again with my level of experience. There still weren't many jobs available, but that didn't stop me from continuing with my search. There were a few companies on a website that were hiring tradesmen. That boosted my confidence. I would *soon* be out of that hell hole. Everything they required, I had. I was more than able to do the tasks they needed done.

I really was hoping that a job would call me back that needed help with work out of town. Those were the jobs I started looking for first. That would be a bonus. They would pay me regularly, on the hour, plus I'd be eligible for overtime, and they'd set me up with a hotel room. And on top of that, they'd pay me per diem every week! Oh, using the company's money to accommodate my lifestyle. Sure. Don't mind if I do. Life couldn't get more glamorous than that. Staying in a wonderful place that hopefully served continental breakfasts in the morning would be a big blessing. The soft, fluffy eggs, homemade waffles, sausages fresh off the stove, a variety of fresh cut fruit, and 100% pure orange juice to wash it all down... then blame it on the breakfast for me being lazy on the job. I'd have plates stacked up in my room so I could come back after work with lustful hunger and devour them. There would be no worries about rent or staying warm, and I could catch up on eating. I looked at the odds as being in my favor. Many people don't like to work out of town because they get homesick, or not wanting to leave family members, or just not having the desire to travel for work.

Not me. Traveling from state to state, or even just being in a state that I hadn't visited before and then staying there for a long time would seem like being born again for me. The only downfall would be if I had to travel on my own dime. Some even had that in the requirements, but I still filled out their applications. I would handle that situation if they ever gave me a chance. My SUV was over 125,000 miles, so that would be risky. It could break down at any moment, and I did not have the funds to cover a repair. My faith was all in the Man upstairs. What is meant to be will come. Now I had something else to fantasize about while I was trying to sleep. Me traveling across the country, or just to a state that I'd never visited before on someone else's dime. That would change my life completely. I had a great feeling it was going to happen. It was like I had already received the call and was just waiting on the date of departure, with my airplane ticket already printed off, and confirmation that a crew would be waiting for me upon my arrival.

The two apartments that I had inquired about didn't come through. *Rejected.* There were still more on my list. I filled out more applications to keep the faith alive. Although I appreciated Labor Forcer for helping me get through my tough times, steady work that made a lot more money was needed. There was another temp agency that a friend told me about, Trades-To-Go Incorporation. They weren't hiring, but I went there anyway and filled out an application. At least they would have me on file for when a job did come up. I wouldn't have to reach out to them, they would call me. I talked to a guy in the office, and he told me there was a job coming up for a street painter. You know the yellow and white lines you see on the interstate and highways? Yeah, someone paints those. They even did parking lots. The only downfall was that it was seasonal. And when it rained, work would be canceled. Paint doesn't stick well to wet surfaces. My plan was to save up all summer long to get back on my feet. It would suck if it rained most of the summer. Tennessee weather is unpredictable. It can be 80 degrees in the afternoon, and by nightfall, it could drop into the 40s. My intentions were to get an electrical job, but once again, life threw me a curve ball. I was doing something totally different. But hey, if it meant steady income—and more of it than before—then it's all cool with me. Besides, the more experience I had in other skills the better my resume would look. But the job was only during summer, so I had to stick it out with Labor Forcer until then.

The jobs were still slow to come in Labor Forcer. The steady work that they did have was mostly stuff workers didn't want, like holding a sign up in front of businesses for promotion. The sign holder position was only on the weekends. I tried it out to earn extra money. I would earn more per hour than on most jobs I was put on, besides being a trashman. The thought of me holding a sign, and somebody that knew me seeing me doing it on a busy intersection would make me feel awkward. But I would only be there for an hour or two, max. It was offered to me before, but I kept turning it down. I had to suck it up and do it. My finances weren't stable enough to be picky. It would be a *major* downgrade from the career I was trying to pursue, but that was in the future. I had to focus on the present. I took the offer, and they sent me to a suburban area to promote a mattress company on Saturday and Sunday. That came as a relief. There would be less chance of being spotted by someone that knew me since I didn't know anyone in that part of town. And my worries about being seen by someone I knew got even smaller when I received the location of my task, which was a whole different city that I rarely ever visited.

On my first day, it rained off and on. I was still getting paid regardless, whether I were indoors shielding myself from the rain or not. There were no flip tricks that went along with it. That part wasn't in my job description. I was just an ordinary guy, holding up an ordinary sign. That was it. Cars would pass by and look, but they didn't get any customers. Not my fault. I tried to stay out there as long as I could without getting soaking wet. A little sprinkle didn't bother me, but when the rain started to pick up, I thought someone would surely signal me to come inside.

There were times the store associates looked out the door and saw it was starting to come down hard, but they just went back to whatever they were doing. I was not about to stand out there looking like a wet dog. I walked straight in and laid down on one of their plush mattresses, after telling them why I came in. They understood. My clothes weren't soaked or dirty, if they had been, I would have found myself a chair to sit in. Right when I got ready to fall asleep, the rain stopped. It happened over and over. There was one time I told myself, "I'm not about to keep coming in and leaving. I will wait until the rain completely stops." On my next break, due to the rain showers, I did just that. Minutes later, I was awoken by one of the store clerks. Yup, that's right. Got caught sleeping on the job. Can you blame me? The sound of the rain outside plus a soft mattress to lay on equals a comfortable rest! Sleep was calling my name, and I took full advantage of it. Sure did. The store didn't have any customers all day. If they were busy, I would've respected their business and done something to stay awake, but since they weren't, I took it upon myself to take a nap. The possibility of getting kicked out of that place or them telling my boss that I was sleeping on the job did cross my mind. If they did tell or had kicked me out for doing such a thing, it wouldn't bother me at all. I didn't plan to do this on a weekly basis anyway. At the end of my shift a lady signed my job slip and asked me if I was coming back the next day. *Yes.* By her wanting me back, she let me know she did not have a problem with me sleeping on the job.

The next day was completely different. There was just one worker operating at the store. The temperature rose tremendously. There were no clouds above, just sun. *Damn, this is about to be a long ass day.* And I was right. That day was awfully long. Two hours would seem like nothing doing regular work, when you're always on the move, but just standing there with a sign like that made time crawl at a snail pace. Granted, I didn't just stand there like a statue, there were times where I went walking up and down the sidewalk with it, but still, it was exhausting. I even tried to make it entertaining by dancing with the sign. I didn't want to at first, but boredom got the best of me. I was willing to do anything to pass the time by. I received a few honks and laughs, but that was it. No potential customers took the bait.

There was a billboard close to me that showed the current temperature and time. I tried my best not to look at the time. When I thought thirty minutes had gone by, only ten had. Sweat started to creep down my chest and back as the sun rays relentlessly beat down on me. It was torture. No one ever told me about any breaks, so I figured since it's just for two hours then maybe they don't recommend you take a break. I didn't bring anything to drink or any food with me. Those items weren't needed really. Shade and a cooling temperature were the only things I wanted. I started to think that it wouldn't hurt to ask if I was allowed to take a break. My body needed a rest from the horrendous heat. Then again, it crossed my mind that she would let me know if I did get a break. I stayed put and waited for the announcement. Though I dressed for the occasion, it was not enough. A whole hour had flown by and the temperature had elevated to what feels like the 90s! *Forget this. I'm about to leave.* That thought kept looping in my head. I want to take a break from the story here to tell you about me being stubborn.

I have always been bull-headed. I like to make my own mistakes and learn from them. Even if someone gives me great advice, I would rather try out my own way first. Only if it potentially, didn't cause a major setback. I wanted to leave so bad, but my ego was stopping me from doing it. If I'd survived the winter months, then surely I could withstand the heat for two hours. Y'all wouldn't understand unless you've been in my shoes. It's one thing to talk about homelessness, but actually experiencing it is something only a few people can endure.

While back on the sidewalk holding a sign for a mattress company, a lady pulled over to the side of the road and hopped out of her car. She must have felt sorry for me baking in the heat like that.

"Hey! Hey!" she said, trying to get my attention," I have some drinks for you. You want some?"

"Yeah."

She then reached inside her car and pulled out a grocery sack full of bottle waters and sodas.

"When I first passed by I was like wow, he's standing out here in this sweltering heat. Then I came back and saw you still standing here. You must be beat."

"Naw, I'm okay, just waiting until it's time to go, which is thirty minutes away."

"Okay, take care of yourself."

"Thanks."

I didn't dare touch the soda. I knew better than that. My stomach would have cramped up something fierce. At the end of my shift, I came to the conclusion that it would be my last time being a sign holder. That was not my thing.

When Monday morning rolled around, I explained to the other workers my experience. One guy said,

"On my breaks, when I was a sign holder, I tried to stay indoors for as long as possible. Sometimes I'd return to work right after my break, but if it was raining like you said, then they would have to tell me to go back out. I wouldn't just be willing to get up and go."

"*What?* You had a break. The spot where I was at didn't have no breaks," I said.

"You're supposed to get a ten-minute break every hour. The office didn't tell you that before you went out there?"

"No, or else I would have taken one."

"What about the people that work there? They didn't tell you either?"

"Nope. The first day I was in and out due to the rain, but Sunday, there was no breaks given and the lady saw me standing outside for two hours straight."

"That couldn't be me. They supposed to tell you you have a break. It's near impossible to be standing out there in this damn heat. Damn near melted the bottom off my boots. Well, you know next time."

"There won't be a next time. I'm tapping out on that job."

The apartments that I applied for the second time were a no-go. I was rejected again! That one hurt, but now, with me working

Monday through Friday as a trashman, maybe I'd have a better shot of landing one. I was taught to always look for the positive in a negative situation. In this case, when I filled out the forms the second time, my work situation wasn't stable. When it came down to how much I made hourly, I put close to the minimum wage at the time—which was $7.25—and since this was an income-based situation, I thought they would have accepted me because at least I was trying to better myself. I was wrong. (It sucks when people reject you just by going off your application and not knowing the real situation behind it. But life goes on, right?) I didn't have the strength to apply for another apartment just to be denied again, so I left it alone until I could prove on my application that my work history was stable. I wanted all my ducks to be lined up in a row. When it was time to fill out another one, they would see I had a stable job even if it were through the temp service, and that would surely get me in the door. I only had to wait and build up experience and a good relationship with the trash company. Maybe, just maybe, they would ask if I wanted to be hired permanently full-time with benefits. It wasn't my ideal job, but when opportunity knocks, you must answer. You never know when it will come back around. From start to finish, my work ethic was fantastic.

I put in months of being a trashman, and it was irking. It was easy and laid back at times, but it just wasn't my cup of tea. I was getting impatient waiting for Trades-To-Go, so I decided to give them a call. To my luck, I received exciting news. The street painters' job started the following week. It had to be close to the end of the week when I made that call. I remembered it being right around the corner. Finally, something positive after all the negativities. "Yes! Yes! I'm done with this."

I was contemplating whether or not to tell my partner the good news. In the end, I didn't say anything. Why? Because, for one, he would have to go to the office anyway to sign in and once he saw that I was no longer signing in, they would easily replace me. And two, I didn't want any peer pressure to come my way begging me to stay. They could have tried to bribe me to stay. My mind was already set on leaving that job. My heart just wasn't in it. It was just something to hold onto so I could show proof of stable work, or until I landed a better job.

My partner was on the other side of the street, working hard getting the trash bags out of people's backyards and putting them on the curbside to be picked up by the truck. I was thinking,

It's gonna suck for him, but I am gone! And I am never coming back. He will have to show someone else the right way to collect trash.

Even if it were somebody new, and even if they had a decent work ethic, he would still have to train them. We were always on a strict time limit to be finished by the end of the day. If we managed it then it was a bonus for the driver, but not for his helpers. It's probably a different situation with other companies, but for this particular one if the driver finished his route before a certain time, he could pick the option to either go home with a full day pay or go back out and help other drivers with their routes which means more time on the clock and more money in his pocket. If only that applied for the temp helper it would've benefited everyone, because then they wouldn't have such a high turnover rate and would get people who took the job more seriously. It was his lucky day when he got assigned me and my partner as his helpers, but all of that was over now.

CHAPTER 11
LIFE OF CURVE BALLS

The first day on my new job at City Paint and Stripe was... interesting. I had stop going to sell my blood plasma since it was on the other side of town where I was working and really didn't need it anymore. The extra money would have been nice, but I didn't regret not going. A guy named Chris, who worked at City Paint and Stripe every season, explained to the new workers that a lot of traveling would be involved,

"Y'all will start off working during the day, but eventually transfer over to nights since it's less traffic."

I had wrecked the company truck. If we had to use our own vehicles, I would have been more cautious because I would have to pay out of my own pocket if I had hit something. Since this was the company's vehicle, the worst thing that could happen was getting fired. I will share more about that accident later in the story.

I was looking forward to getting out and going to different cities I'd never seen. Lord knows, I needed a break. With clear skies and the sun shining, that is what I call a good start for something new. It was a big step above every job I was assigned to when working for Labor Forcer. The daily task was simple. Every day before we headed out for work, the paint truck had to be filled up. The paint comes in powder form, in plastic bags. There are two tanks on the truck - one for the yellow paint, and the other for the white that you see on the interstates, highways, and parking lots. The hardest part was to keep the tanks filled up and that was the task assigned to whoever rode on the back of the truck. It really wasn't hard, but compared to everything else, it was top of the list. You didn't have to rip the bag open to pour in the powder paint. You could just throw the whole thing in the tank and the actuator would rip it open, then the hot steam melts the powder and turns it into liquid. There were three trucks total. The two escort vehicles were regular pick-up trucks. One drove in front of the paint truck, and one followed up behind to stop traffic from interfering with the fresh paint that was being put down. Chris was training me on driving. This was a simple, kick back type of job. It didn't matter what you were doing. Everything was laid back until it came time to fill up the tanks again, which meant hauling multiple fifty-pound bags. The first job we did was a couple of miles away and we got it done quick, so nobody got a full day's pay on our first day. That sucked, because I needed all the money I could get. Since I was trained on what to do when driving the truck, on the second day I had one of the escort trucks all to myself. The window was down, and the radio was blasting with me jamming out to every song.

There was one spot we went to that I will never forget. It was somewhere far away from Nashville. There was a river flowing under the bridge, with mountains nearby. I took it as the sign of a breakthrough. The sun shining down on the water made it glitter. It was peaceful. Everything that I had been going through, all the long days and even longer nights, it all disappeared as I was hypnotized by my surroundings. I said to myself, "This is what I call true peace." I stayed there for thirty minutes before it was time for us to move to the next spot. We traveled to some local cities, but most were outside of Nashville. To me, it was a vacation. To others, it was work.

As time went on, I got used to everything quick. It was a no-brainer when I was getting prepared for that day's work. Traveling to the countryside was my favorite. It was not as congested as the city. Looking out at all that open road and acres upon acres of green land helped widen my imagination. When you're homeless, it's easy to be sucked up in a hopeless way of thinking and feel like you're never going to get out and like nobody cares about you or wants to lend a hand to help. It was hard to keep applying for housing and keep getting turned down. My trick was to explore new things and places to help take my mind off the negativity. It helped. After work, I would return to the same old reality of sleeping in my vehicle, but always looking forward to the next day when I could step back into fantasy land. It was like my escape.

A comparison to that is when people get fed up with relationships, a job, or whatever the case might be. Sometimes they take a vacation, mostly to the mountains. In Tennessee, Gatlinburg is where people go who want to escape their own personal world of chaos or to relax. The high altitude gives you a sense of peace and comfort as you gaze out your cabin window or, better yet, while you sit in a hot tub and look out over God's creation that blankets you with beauty. That's the feeling I'm referring to when I was taking trips to unfamiliar places. My personal vacation on the company's dime.

After a couple of months working during the day, it was the night shift from there on out. I always looked forward to the *Quiet Storm* segment that played on *92Q* radio station while I drove at night. The good ole oldies. Our new start time was 7pm. When the music switched from oldies to gospel, that was the indicator that our shift was almost over, which usually was around three o'clock in the morning. It began to be a struggle, driving all night like that and trying to stay awake while doing so. We usually didn't get back to the shop until sunrise. It was a fight to travel far out like that, driving all night and trying to stay awake on the way back. Nothing seemed to help. I tried letting down the window so the frigid air would keep me awake, but it was too damn cold in the mornings, so I preferred the window to stay up. I tried turning up the radio. That became too annoying because they would play songs I didn't like or know. Then life had to throw another curve ball into the mix. Day after day, it kept raining and raining.

Like I said before, there was no painting work when it rained. And the same was true if it had rained before the start of the shift, because the streets would still be wet and so my boss would cancel work for that day. There were times we would pull up on the area where paint was needed, and it would start raining. We would sit around to see if it would pass. Sometimes it was a little drizzle, which was okay. A light drizzle would not stop us from accomplishing our goal for that day. The one time it rained so hard that we had to pack up, I asked the boss if there was another spot we could go to get a full day's pay and come back to that area later. The other job was stretched so far out that it would be impossible to leave one area and get to the next in time. There was no chance of completing it before it was time to clock out. That company wasn't overtime friendly. There were some instances it gave us some, but it was not a common thing.

On the consecutive weeks where it didn't rain, the money was flowing in great. I could pay for a motel room on a weekly basis. A big jump for me. My goal was to save as much money as possible because this was only a seasonal thing, so I couldn't get too relaxed by eating fast food every day and night. It was on one of the days when I did get too relaxed that I wrecked the company truck.

Now that I had a steady income, with proven stability at work, I could present my paystubs to the government housing department. There was only one that I applied for which required me to go into the office for an interview. No problem at all. I went to my storage unit and pulled out some khakis and a collared shirt and clean shoes. I was prepared to give them thanks for accepting my resident application. I had my resume and work contacts ready to go. On the application, under the homeless part, it had two selections to choose from. The first one was staying on the street, and the second was living in a vehicle. I picked the second one, of course. Then it was time for me to fill out my income situation. I filled it out and had my check stubs in hand with my social security card, in case they needed to make copies. I said to myself, "This is it. I know it," The first applications didn't require an interview. They were just applications that you filled out online, but at this one they could really see the real me.

The wait wasn't long for the interview. Once I sat down and spoke with the lady, I told her the truth about me being homeless and hoped she could relate to where I was coming from. Hopefully, she would see that I was out working hard and trying my best to live a normal life. I was on another level from most people that were applying, and my appearance was decent.

After my interview, she handed over my application to the manager for review. I was confident that they were going to give me guidelines on my first apartment. I sat there and waited patiently. The interviewer called me back up. I whispered, "Oh boy, this is it."

"I'm sorry to tell you, but your application was rejected."

"How is that? I'm homeless."

"The manager looked it over and saw that you made too much money on the hour."

"Sorry."

"Well, can I talk to him myself?"

"No one is allowed in the back, but workers and only if he request to see someone."

I tried over and over, pleading with the lady that I really needed this, but it wasn't up to her. It was the manager who declined it, and there was no way of having a one-on-one conversation with him. I was making $13 per hour. After paying my rent at the motel, gas, and food for the week, I was left with barely enough to get by, and on top of that, there still was a car note hanging over my head that I wasn't paying, but at least the main necessities were taken care of.

"I'm sorry. There is other government housing you can apply for."

"Okay," I said, and left the room with my head down.

That was supposed to be income-based properties. But even with income and proof of steady work, they still rejected me. That outcome was not what I expected. I got in my SUV and pulled off. My heart was crushed. Tears began to form overflowing my cheeks.

"Even though it sucks, I still believe in you God."

That was all I could say. There was no turning back. At that point, I still had to believe there was better for me in store, or my mind would have been blank on what to do next. I threw in the towel on looking for somewhere to stay. The motel was cool, but an actual apartment would have been better, and even though I was thinking about getting a place in the projects, I felt as if I were now too good for it. The steady income I had could mean a better living environment, and plus the waiting list for a place in the projects was usually months out. Pregnant ladies or single mothers, most of the time, get pulled to the top of the list is what I was told. At least I still had a job, a motel room that came with a *real* bed with sheets, a TV, and A/C.

It was an ordinary day at work. We were all inside, sitting in the meeting room waiting for our shift to begin. We were talking and joking around as usual. After I clocked in, my plan was to follow the same daily routine - drive all the company trucks from inside the shop to the outside parking lot. But this day was different. The first truck I hopped in was the boss's, which he would normally drive when he was not driving the paint truck. With the key in the ignition, I started it up and put it in drive. Still in my comfort state, I didn't notice how close the other vehicle was parked right next to me. I began to pull out and turned the wheel way too soon. *Screeeeeeeeeeeech!* "What the hell was that?!" I looked over to my left rear-view mirror and didn't see anything. Looked over to the right and saw the truck was rubbing up against the other truck that was parked next to it. Nobody was around when it happened. They were still in the room. I got out and checked the damage, trying to see if I could fix the problem. My eyes got big when I saw how bad the damage was. The truck that was next to me had only minor scratches and dents. That was an old vehicle anyway. No one came out immediately. But my boss's truck had a big dent on the side of it. I backed the truck back into its spot and quickly thought of a plan. *Maybe I can fake like this was done before I got here.* Not a second later, before I thought of a lie, my co-workers started to come out. In the back of my head, I was thinking, *Well, it's been nice working here. I'm fired fosho. First, I didn't get accepted for any housing... Now this. Damn mannn!* The crew started inspecting the damages. I didn't think the sound was that loud. No bosses were around, just the crew members. It wouldn't be kept a secret for long though, eventually the boss would know. Either he would fire me or give me a second chance. There was no excuse that I could have come up with. I was the only one in the truck, and there were no distractions around. Hitting a parked truck made me seem foolish, "How could I be so stupid and not pull out far enough to make the turn? I'd pulled the damn truck out plenty of times before with no issues. Why today? Why me?"

After the crew leader Chris looked closely at the beat-up truck, he gave me some peace of mind.

"Aw, this just a fender bender. It ain't that bad."

"Will they fire me though?"

"I don't think so. That's why they have insurance on all their vehicles, for potential wrecks such as head-on collisions, but not someone hitting a parked vehicle."

The whole team started laughing, but I didn't think it was funny. My job was on the line and they didn't know how much it meant to me because of my personal situation. Without this job, I'd be back at square one just when I was getting ahead.

"Look here. It's better if you tell the boss yourself than try to hide it like nothing happened and have him find out on his own. You feel me?"

"Yeah. You think he will be mad?"

"Naw, well… I don't know. This the first time this happened. What I do know is people will give you a hard time about it by making jokes."

"I don't care about that. All I'm worried about is if I can keep my job. This is a cool laid-back job."

The mechanic got in the truck and pulled it outside himself. Minutes later, there was the boss. There we were, having a stare-off at each other. There was no turning back now.

"You see your truck over there? Guess who did it?" a co-worker said.

I was just thinking, like, *well damn, he didn't even give me a chance to come clean.*

"Yeah," he said, as he stared me dead in the eyes. "I already heard. Y'all make sure the trucks get a full tank of gas and start prepping for tonight."

Everyone else headed out while I stayed back. I figured he didn't want to fire me in front of everyone. I braced myself for the sad news to come. He walked straight past me, heading for the office to look at the job board for that night without saying a single word to me. As he passed, I apologized, which he did acknowledge. I left and started helping others prep for the night shift.

"What he say?"

"Was he mad?"

"Did he fire you?"

"Naw. He was cool with it. I know he's upset, but not to the point he wanted to fire me."

"I told you," said Chris. "They can fix that dent, and they don't have to call their insurance to file a claim. The truck is still drivable, and that was the main issue."

Chris said that I would be the joke of the day, and he was right. For at least half of that shift my crew was clowning me. At first it didn't bother me. At least I still had my job, and I was somewhat prepared for it. Then I started to get annoyed, and they could feel my energy. That's when the jokes ended.

The next day when we came in, I saw how they fixed it. You could still see where the damage occurred, but it looked better than it did. I dodged a big bullet there. You better believe from that point forward that I was extremely careful pulling out. A couple of days later, one of the team members reversed into a guard rail and bent it backwards. It was all laughter in his case. We were parked at an abandoned lot. The truck he was driving was too big for that guard rail to cause any damages to it. He didn't even notice he'd hit it until somebody told him to stop, otherwise he would have kept going. The boss saw him in action but didn't get mad. The guardrail was destroyed, but it only caused minor damage to the truck. Nobody was clowning him for hitting something like they did me, *where is the equal treatment*?

My Ford Explorer started to overheat one day. I took it into a mechanic shop to see what the problem was. The housing on my thermostat had gone bad. After being quoted over $200 to fix it, I decided to walk away. It wouldn't stay overheated for long. It would fluctuate back and forth. Since it didn't stay overheated, like a blown head gasket or bad water pump, I didn't worry about it as much as I should have.

I took it to one of the auto parts stores to see if they could fill me in on what it would take to fix the problem. The part I needed was under $30 when the cashier pulled it up on the computer.

"Cool. I thought it would be more expensive than that. Is it something that I could fix myself? I don't have the money to pay a mechanic."

"Yeah, you have your vehicle here?"

"It's parked right outside."

"Okay, let me show you how to change it out."

I opened the hood.

"This is your housing right here. It's just these three bolts. You take them out and remove the housing. Reverse the process with the new one, and you're good to go."

"For real?! That's it?"

"Yup, easy just like that. If you don't have the tools to take the bolts off, we can lend you ours. What did they quote you?"

"Too much."

I pulled the receipt out of my pocket and handed it to him.

"This is unbelievable!" He said.

He held onto it and showed the other guys in the store. They were amazed also by the crazy price.

"They can charge you up to a certain percentage of the retail," said a guy who overheard the conversation," It sucks, but it's legal."

"For something I can fix myself, in less than ten minutes for only $30?"

"Yup, and for labor it's typically around $75 an hour, so that's probably why it spiked up so high."

Since it wasn't going to break my pockets, I had bought the part and put it on myself instead of paying the ridiculous cost for parts and labor. It was a win-win situation for me. The part was cheap, and I saved a lot of money by doing it myself. Everything was working fine. After two days, I decided to put the old part back on and keep the new one inside the SUV. You're probably wondering why. It wouldn't stay overheated for long, so I thought the old one was good enough until it finally went out completely, and when it did, I could replace it with the new one. Obviously I wasn't thinking straight.

One day when I walked out of my motel room to start it up, the engine wouldn't start. I turned the key again, still no chance of it starting. I put the new part back on. Still nothing. That was the weekend when my SUV decided to die on me. That got me thinking I should have left the new part on there to begin with, or maybe it had nothing to do with that. Maybe it was something else that I wasn't aware of. I had a little bit of money still saved up enough to get somebody to come and give me a diagnostic report on it. I decided to call a mobile mechanic to check it out. His price was decent enough not to burn a hole in my pocket. Hopefully, he could tell me something that I could fix myself without the labor cost. That was something I couldn't afford. I gave him a call, and when he came to check it out, it turned out to be something that he would have to pull the whole engine out to fix. After he said that, I knew it was going to be over my budget. *How am I going to get to work now?*

The city bus was one of my options. The problem with that was I could get a ride to work, but the time I got off in the morning was before the buses started running. And the only hope I had of getting a ride to and from work was if we worked overtime. Working overtime would give me a better chance of the buses running by the time I arrived back at the shop. But that wasn't guaranteed, or even likely, because we barely worked any extra hours. My other option would be better but would cost more money - renting a car. For how long? I didn't know the answer to that, but I still had to get to work somehow to maintain my steady income.

I decided to ride the city bus and pick up a rental at the airport. It was money going down the drain, but there was no other possibility to guarantee that I would get to and from work. I rented it out for a week. While the job was only seasonal, my real occupation—being an electrician—was where my focus needed to be. There are a lot of people who have degrees and aren't even pursuing the career field they studied for. That wasn't going to be me. There were still months left on the painting job, but I knew better than to wait till the last minute before looking for work. If I could start applying now, there would be a greater chance of me landing an electrical job before my time was up with the painting company. After spending all that money to rent out a vehicle for a full week, my decision was to sleep in the car and not the motel. That's right, back to the Piggly Wiggly parking lot. It was a tradeoff. I simply couldn't afford to sleep comfortably and rent out a car. I gained in one area and had to sacrifice the other. It was only after I returned the rental back that I would allow myself to go back to the motel.

While I was in the parking lot, waiting on time to pass by, I reminisced on all the things that'd led up to this situation. Boy, it had been a struggle, and I didn't know how long it would be before I could live freely again. Then it hit me, right as I was reading a chapter out of my Bible. Never had I thought about living my life like I was. Everything I had been through seemed like a movie. Then I felt as if God spoke to my spirit,

"You can't have a *movie* without the book first."

It made so much sense. Movies usually evolve from books. I normally don't read books, let alone write them. You couldn't pay me enough to read a whole chapter book back then, and now here I am writing my second! Never in my life had being an author become a part of my thought process. This is crazy! If I could help others by sharing my story, then I had to do it. Plus, it would be mined blowing to the people that know me to hear about my story. Nobody in my life ever knew what was going on, not my family or even friends, but now they will after reading this. There's still a lot more to take in.

I thought about recording my events day-by-day, with the exact dates listed out so I wouldn't miss out on any juicy details. Already months had passed since I'd come up with the idea. Some of the events I could recall and others I couldn't. When it came time for me to write my first book: *Lost in My World*, it contained the events that came to mind which were most important since they were embedded deepest in my thoughts.

After work, I thought about an electrical company, Duewell Electric, that a friend told me about a while back. Apparently, they were always hiring. I decided to give them a call to see if that was true. The receptionist confirmed they were hiring and to come in to fill out an application. I had my college portfolio nice and neat ready to present if there was going to be an interview that same day. Everyone should know the famous quote by now,

"If you stay ready, you never have to get ready."

That portfolio had all my technical college academics and some pictures that showed me doing hands-on training to separate me from all the other candidates.

The head of safety, Jim, came to see me. I thought I would fill out the application and leave. But he stayed, and we had more of a casual conversation than a formal interview. He was impressed as he looked over my portfolio.

"Wow! No one ever bought a portfolio with them. This looks great."

"Thanks. I'm just trying to separate myself from the average Joe."

"I hear ya. When are you looking to start?"

"Next Monday."

"Someone will give you a call tomorrow."

"Okay," I said and left.

Now it was time for me to play the wait *patiently* "game." Him telling me someone will give me a call back made me think I landed the job. This was the first interview ever that I heard that, but still was unsure what to think. Meanwhile, I was trying to get my head wrapped around how I was going to get back and forth to work. I couldn't rent out a car forever. My mind was clueless. The only thing I knew how to do was keep going and hope something would fall into place soon.

My vehicle broke down. The rental I was in was temporary, and so was the motel. I waited days for a returned call from Duewell Electric. I called them to check the status of my application. Jim answered and told me someone should have already called, and that he would see what the delay was about. He let me know that I would for sure get a call back before the day's end. Minutes later, I got the call and the answer I had been searching for. Someone from the Human Resource (H.R) Department told me the location, time, and date—that Monday coming up—to be at the job site. After hanging up I said to myself, "I'm back where I need to be finally."

I started to plan out my route. The city bus would drop me off a block away from where I worked, but I knew that was kind of sketchy. I had to catch the very first city bus, and sometimes they were on a different schedule. For instance, if there was a big event downtown where some of the streets were blocked off, that would cause me to be late. If the driver didn't pull up to the bus stop on time, that too could cause me to be late.

City Paint and Stripe was an excellent job that I didn't want to leave. I asked my boss if I could work out a deal where I could maintain both jobs. Our work sometimes went on all night, until the morning when my electrical job was about to start. There was no way I could have gotten off early just to make it on time for Duewell Electric. Nobody could leave early, unless someone met up with them in the same city we were doing work in. A few times, we would travel an hour away from Nashville. We always left our vehicles at the office and moved to different spots on a day-to-day basis. My boss told me straight up,

"Either you work here, or you work somewhere else. There is no leaving early to go to another job, and we're not going to work around your schedule."

"Okay, this will be my last week then."

"Okay."

I was going to make it a habit to put back a certain amount of money from each check to buy me a car flat out. Cash is "king" in the car business. With cash, it's easier to negotiate prices than when you only have money for a downpayment.

My mother gave me the blueprint on buying cars when I bought my first one, a red 2000 Chevy Cavalier. It wasn't the car I had dreamt about, but it came with no car payments. This situation wouldn't be no different. I needed temporary transportation. Once I had saved up enough, I could buy a decent car that would get me from A to Z. Then I could save up to trade it in for a better one. Obviously, I didn't have enough money to pay the full price, so I would have to go against the grain and finance one. But that would be better than riding the city bus, which was usually overcrowded.

The rental set my finances back, but not too much. There were plenty of car lots on Dickerson Road, near my motel, so I went window shopping for cars. There were so many to visit, but one lot in particular caught my eye. It had the car that I wanted ever since high school - a white 2002 Nissan Maxima that came with black tints. The salesman, who also was the owner, was cool. We had a very brief discussion about my job history and what I was earning. The car was set to the side and looked like it had been sitting there for quite a while. My emotions got the best of me. Looking for a reliable vehicle went straight out the window, and I had to have it as is, regardless of whether the motor was about to fall out. I didn't have enough money for the down payment we agreed on, but told him I would definitely be back.

My days with the rental were up. The next day, I called up Druski to drop me off at work. He did. I knew it wouldn't be an everyday thing. And him picking me back up, I can forget about it. I arrived back at the shop early in the morning which was usually around 4 or 5am. I knew he wasn't coming to get me that early, so there was no reason for me to ask.

Around two in the morning, it started to rain. My only hope was it stopping suddenly, so we could continue to work, but it didn't.

We headed back to the shop. I asked one of my co-workers who was traveling in the same direction if he could drop me off at my motel after work. It was literally right off the interstate where he dropped me off before. My request was denied. His priority was to rush home to see his girlfriend, who probably was still in bed sleeping. We made it back to the shop, and it was still hours before sunrise. He parked the company truck. I sat there for a second. Life started to strangle me again. My eyes began to water, and he noticed.

"Are you going to be okay?"

If he only knew how much pain I was holding in due to life constantly beating me down and not being able to vent to anyone, he wouldn't have dared to ask me that. And he knew I didn't have a ride. I wiped my eyes before a tear dropped.

"Yeah," I said before opening up the door and getting out.

I was too embarrassed to ask anyone else cause they would know that I'm staying at a motel. So, in my mind they would know that I'm homeless. He was a person that I knew wasn't going to judge me. Everyone else, I wasn't so sure about.

Everybody was getting in their cars and leaving. I was the last one to go. I stood back pretending I was doing extra things before I left. I didn't want anyone to see me walking. The motel was miles away from my location. The only thing that could get me there was my two legs, two feet, and pure determination. I began the long walk and made it to the motel safely.

I'm not the prideful type. I don't like to be a burden to anyone, that's why I keep things to myself. It helps me handle the fear of being rejected when there really comes a time that I need help. Like this situation.

That Friday, luck was on my side, Druski gave me a ride to work and we finished late enough that I could catch the city bus back to my motel. I broke the news to my boss before leaving that that was my last day working there. "This isn't my career choice, being an electrician is." He understood. I got my check and bounced to catch the city bus and head to my room.

I walked to the car lot, half a mile away from the motel, hoping to drive a car back. I had already cashed my check and was willing to hand over the money to him without hesitation, but he told me he had to check out other things on the car. He was completely honest. He couldn't just take my money and say good luck with it. It was his integrity he had to protect.

"This car been sitting here for a long time. I'm not sure what all is wrong with it."

"I don't care. This the car I want. Here is the down payment. It starts up, right?"

"Yeah."

"It goes forward and backwards, right?"

"Yeah."

"It is fine."

"No, no, no, you just don't hand your money over without knowing anything about the car first."

I knew that, but this was a desperate situation. This was the car I had wanted for a long time, and I was stuck with a broken-down vehicle.

"You give me till Monday, and I will have it ready by the time you get off work."

"But I need it to get to work."

"You can always ride the city bus."

I sensed he wasn't going to budge, and I'm glad he didn't. There was a possibility that the car could be a lemon.

"Waiting till Monday is days away, but okay."

"Okay, it will be ready by then."

CHAPTER 12
BACK ON TRACK

The night before the start of my new job was exciting. I tried my best to go to sleep but couldn't. It was hard for me to trust the city bus to get me to work on time. It would be my first day, and I would hate for it to start with telling my boss that the city bus made me late. There was too much at stake to take that chance. That whole night, I stayed up until it was time for me to leave and walk to the jobsite. My job started at 7am, but I wanted to be there 30 minutes early to take a break before I clocked in, and I knew it was going to be a hassle getting there by walking with all my tools plus an umbrella since it was raining outside. I decided to leave at 4am. The job was a few miles away. I gave myself plenty of time to make it. "Whewwww! This one will be for the history books," I said to myself. There was no turning back. I had to continue forward with my decision. I had a permanent job, and not only that, but it was in the career field that I had chosen. Things were starting to get on track and stay there, *finally!* One thing was for certain, I would have a car waiting for me when I got off. That was another motivational tip that kept me going. I had my drill case and tool bag in one hand, and an umbrella in the other. Now it was time for me to use nothing but my two feet to get me to my destination.

It was miserable. It rained off and on. I had on a big black coat to shield me from getting drenched, but at times, it began to get hot under it. There were times I took it off when the rain stopped, then I'd put it back on when the downpour came back with vengeance. I made it half a mile down the street when I was stopped by the police. He flashed his lights and pulled into a parking lot nearby, wanting me to come over. I kept walking because I wasn't doing anything wrong. Me walking down the street so early in the morning might have seemed odd, but again, no crime was being committed. I heard his car door open,

"Hey!"

I kept walking.

"Hey, I'm talking to you!"

"What I do?"

"I just want to talk to you right quick."

I have nothing to hide, and maybe he would give me a ride the rest of the way to work, I thought.

"Where you going?"

"To work. I'm an electrician."

"Where are you working at?"

"Near downtown Nashville. It's a new addition they are adding onto a university and today will be my first day."

Many questions were being asked, and I answered them truthfully. He was really starting to make me angry. There I was, just trying to make it to work on time, trying to better my life, when I hit this roadblock that was about to make me late on my first day. He got on his radio and asked for assistance. The other cop showed up minutes later.

"Here's the deal. There have been a lot of burglaries in this area, and you with all these tools, walking down the street, at this time of morning, seem suspicious."

I knew my rights. Looking suspicious is not a crime, but I wasn't going to get into an argument with them about it. I just wanted to make it to work on time. The other officer asked similar questions, and I gave him the same answers. After their shenanigans, I wanted to see if they would make all this worth the time they'd wasted. I looked back and forth at both of them in their eyes when I asked this question.

"Well, since y'all know I'm not a thief, could one of y'all take me to work? It's not that far from here if you drive."

"*Psssh,* were not a taxicab. We have work to do ourselves."

"Okay, am I good to go now?"

"Yeah. Good luck."

Man that was messed up. With all that time wasted, my anxiety started kicking in. I was going to be late. I could almost bet that there weren't really a lot of burglaries going on. He wanted a good excuse to see what I was doing, which was minding my own business. After they were out of my sight, I began jogging to try to get back the time I'd lost. Carrying all that stuff while wearing a big coat was exhausting. It wasn't even cold outside, but that was the only coat that I had. One minute it would rain, so I'd stop jogging, put on my coat, and then continue. Then the rain would stop and I would have to stop jogging to take it off. I got so tired of doing that, sometimes I would just let myself get wet from whatever rain the umbrella didn't catch. I just had to protect my tools from getting wet.

When I made it downtown, I was halfway there. The sun was beginning to rise, and my body was out of energy. I had to sacrifice a couple of minutes of down time to get my wind back. It felt good sitting on the curb like that, taking a break, without the rain coming down of course. There was still a goal I had to accomplish. I got back up and proceeded forward, with a mixture of jogging and fast walking. If it wasn't for me being optimistic that I was going to get my car after work, I don't think I would have been able to do that. He gave me his word that it would be done when I got off. I gave myself a motivational speech,

"It's just for this one time. After work today, I will start driving in."

I made it to the job site an hour prior to starting time. I talked with one of the guys from the construction office to see if I was at the right spot. "Yes," he said. I sat in one of the chairs outside to decompress. I tried to regain all my energy before work started. My shirt was soaked, more from sweat than rain. I took off my boots, my coat, laid my tools beside me, and chilled out until the start of my shift. That was a hard challenge for me. All I could think of was how it had better be my last time doing it. I wouldn't be able to do it two days in a row. If that's the case, I would have to depend on the city bus to get me to work on time. It was time for me to meet up with my co-workers. I was wishing my first day would be easy and laid back. I was still tired, but did my best to act like nothing was wrong.

My first personal assignment was to get some water back into my system that I had sweated out, then I could work. After doing that, the electrician I was helping, Oscar, told me to get a bundle of three-quarter conduit from outside. It was a bundle of 10 ten-foot lengths of pipe. I took a deep breath and went outside to get it. It was tough picking up that bundle of pipe, but I muscled it and brought it in.

"I said three-quarter, not one inch."

It had been a while since I'd done electrical work, so I had to refresh my memory. I was still new to it all, even though I had months of prior experience. I forgot the conduit sizes are written on the conduit. After bringing in the right bundle, he then told me to go back outside and get a ladder. *Oh boy, today is not going to be easy.* Over time, my body gained back its strength. Better believe on my morning and afternoon break I was in a spot alone, with my boots off, sleeping. The rest of the workday went fine, with no complaints of me being too tired to do anything.

After I clocked out for the day, I imagined myself driving in my white 2002 Nissan Maxima going wherever and whenever I wanted. As I approached the bus stop, my boss pulled up on me to talk,

"Do you want a ride?"

"Naw, the bus coming soon."

"You sure?"

"Yeah, I don't want you going out of your way."

"It's fine. Where you need to go?"

It would really help get me there quicker before the car lot closes, but I didn't want him to know I was staying at a motel. Then I thought, he didn't have to drop me off there, he could drop me off where my car was. I gave him the destination, and he took me there. As we pulled up, I saw my car sitting up front and center. It was cleaned up, looking nice, and running. I thanked my boss for the ride, and he left. I went inside to take care of the paperwork. After that, off I went with my new car that I had been waiting so long for. My only option was to sleep in the back of that car since I had a payment to make on it every month.

The job wasn't paying me that much, since I was still fresh to the trade. My position was electrician helper. College taught me some things, but it's better to learn more on the job itself by getting your hands dirty. It seemed strange at first, having a permanent job and steady income like that but still sleeping in my car. It was a means of survival. The spring season was great. When I got off, it was sometimes cloudy with a little breeze to help smooth out my day. People were always talking about what they were going to do after work. I never included myself in that conversation, but if I happened to be asked what I would do I generally responded with, "chilling as usual." That was the truth. I would be chilling all right, being bored inside my car. My options were to either take a nap in the stadium parking lot after work, or sit in the park somewhere until night fall. The best days were when it rained. The sound of the rain tapping on my windshield softly would help me fall asleep. I would crack my windows to get the cool air to circulate, but sometimes that meant the rain would start dripping in the car. How hard it was raining would change how high I rolled up my windows. It was bad when I had to roll my windows all the way up, leaving me stuck inside a hot stuffy car. The summer season was the worst. Although I let down my windows, the inside of my car still felt like it was ninety degrees while the sun was beaming down on it, baking me. Those were some very miserable moments. There was no chance of me leaving the car running while I took a nap. I wasn't going to waste my gas like that, so I had to suck it up and just look forward to another day.

As time went on, I became better at being an electrician helper. I hadn't earned the title of an electrician yet, but I was on track to become one. To technically earn that title you had to complete the apprenticeship program and on-the-job training. Then you would earn the official title of a Journeyman Electrician. Many people call themselves an electrician because they've been in the trade for years and know what they are doing without having supervision. I think it's best to have experience on the job mixed in with a little education. School doesn't teach you everything, but having completed it did help me get my foot in the door with my first electrical contractor. I wanted to separate myself from the pack. That's why I went to tech college to get my diploma. Duewell Electric offered to pay a portion of my apprenticeship school as part of their benefits package. If you kept a C average in all the years you attend—which is four—then you would not have to pay the full amount. The time had not yet arrived for me to sign up, but when it did come, I would be looking to take full advantage of that opportunity.

I began to build a strong name for myself. Whenever there was overtime offered, I would be the first to volunteer. Little did they know, I literally didn't have anything else to do after work. No responsibilities, no running errands, no hanging out with friends, nothing! I am a great worker. For weeks and weeks consecutively, I always volunteered to do overtime. If I had been financially stable back then, I would have still stayed late or come in on the weekends, but not as much as I was doing.

I sensed jealousy in the air. My boss was bragging about how much of a hard worker I was. Oscar and others started to catch on. If the electrician I was helping needed some materials or a tool, usually I would already have it in my hands waiting for them to grab it. I constantly had people tell me to slow down. They were wanting to stretch out the day with their current tasks, but being just helper I felt like I was on the chopping block. I had to prove myself. If I got caught slacking, I feared that my supervisor would give me the boot and tell me to never return to that jobsite.

The first person I had an issue with was Oscar. Then someone else, then someone else. It got to the point that nobody wanted to work with me. I know a lot of people experience that at their workplace. The first thing I did was check myself. "Did my attitude need adjustment? No. Was I doing the tasks that were given to me? Yeah." I made a few mistakes, sure, but nothing out of the ordinary and nothing that cost the company a large amount of money to fix. I came to the conclusion it was their problem and not mines. Some of my mistakes were the same ones everyone else was making too. I tried to pay attention to every single thing that the electricians were doing, so when it came time for me to do those things I would know what to do. Like my first electrical job, I wasn't going to let anyone bully me just because I wasn't as experienced as them. I stood up for myself when the time was right, and held my tongue when I didn't want to. Once my "back-off" meter reached its highest point, I let my words experience freedom. My mouth expressed what I'd been holding back. What you give, is what you receive. There was never a point where me and Oscar were screaming and yelling at each other, only a few choice words were exchanged.

Why are people like that? Whenever I was helping another electrician, I always got whatever materials they wanted. It didn't matter how far I had to walk to get them, as long as I was respected. When there was no respect given, I would express my thoughts about the situation freely and either help out someone else or do a task alone that I knew needed to be done. It was a company full of foreigners, and I was the only Black guy working on that specific jobsite. It felt like they were either trying to get me fired or get me to quit. Me being a quitter was out of the question, especially over some knuckle head that didn't like it when I stood up for myself. If I was going to quit, it would be for a better job. Not because I couldn't stand the people I worked with. That was a challenge to me, and I gladly accept challenges. That is what builds character. Being in a workplace where most of your team don't like you and still not quitting is, in my opinion, telling them I am much stronger than they are. But there are also situations when your time has run out on a job and the next step is to look elsewhere. This was not on that level. When they were mean to me, I tried to be kind back. It was a challenge for me to do, so that's what I was working on whenever negativity was thrown my way. Be kind to those who are not kind to you. I get it, but I still spoke my mind when they pushed me to the edge.

In the beginning, I had no choice but to bite my tongue. I had been searching for a permanent job for a long time. Even if I did get fired, that wouldn't disappoint me too much. I was still living out of my car. It couldn't get any worse than that. But since I had landed the job, I knew I had come too far to go back now, and besides, apprenticeship schooling was coming up.

This was different from Miller-Motte Technical College which I had graduated from. This was to be a certified *Journeyman Electrician.* With that card, I could negotiate better wages. My trade school diploma showed how serious I was about making this my career, and it's what got me in the door with my first electrical company, but that's all it did. It was time to take it a step further and graduate from another school to be an electrician and not stay as a helper. My credits would transfer over to that school once I enrolled. That meant instead of doing four years, I only had to do two. And even less than that if I went to summer classes.

Some guys at work were sharing their opinions about apprenticeship schooling to people that were looking at getting their certified electrician card. One after another chimed in,

"It's not worth it."

"School don't matter, it is the on-the-job experience what counts."

"It's only a card they give you, not an actual license."

"Companies don't care about that."

Everyone that was going to attend the apprenticeship school wasn't going to budge on what the experienced electricians thought. They were the ones without electrician cards. As for me, it was my way of making a better lifestyle. Without that card that said I was a certified electrician, would be hard to negotiate pay. The interviewer could use that as one of the reasons not to pay me what I'm worth. The top out pay in your last year of apprenticeship was $18 back in 2016. The electricians that were in the field a long time but didn't obtain the card weren't getting what they were worth either. I wasn't about to wait five or more years to top out like that, versus topping out in just a couple of years of schooling.

CHAPTER 13
SLOW DOWN! SLOW DOWN!

When the fall season came back around, I received a huge blessing. In the mornings, on my way to work, I would hear Steve Harvey share his motivational speeches before the actual podcast came on. It helped guide me through my heartache. Sometimes, it felt as if he was talking directly to me being that we share similar life stories. He had been homeless too. He had lived in his car. The things he would discuss would hit home, and I knew that on the other side of that storm was a beautiful day.

On construction jobs, when men see a lady they would all stop what they were doing to have a look at what might be eye candy. As I was working on the top floor of this building, Oscar looked out the window and spotted two ladies making their way inside, carrying cleaning supplies. From far back it wasn't much to look at, so I didn't pay it no mind. I went on with my day as usual.

The first couple of days I saw no sign of them. Then one day, there they were, being friendly to everyone. They were the type of ladies that wouldn't hurt a fly but will kill germs. I didn't speak when I came across them like everybody else did. I felt as if a dark cloud was hanging over me. I hardly ever spoke to anyone. I would be too tired in the mornings from not getting enough sleep at night from tossing and turning in the front seat. They were the complete opposite of each other. One was energetic, and the other seemed laid back. Every time they walked pass me, there was no communication involved. The same goes for when I walked pass them. I did notice that one had a black girl booty, and she was far from being black. Very few people knew her name, but those who didn't refer to her as,

"The lady with the big butt," and you automatically knew which lady they were talking about. The other had very large breasts. Together, they were a real dynamic duo of friendly individuals. I would have never thought they would play such a *significant role* in my life.

My friend Tim's dad died. His dad's house was already paid for, but he didn't want to live in it. I asked him if it was okay for me to stay there. No rent was discussed. He handed me over a copy of the keys, and that's when I knew it was for real. The only downside was I had to pay off the bills… water, gas, and electric. The only bill that would be a challenge to pay off was the gas bill, which was around $600. The gas was cut off until the past due balance was paid. All of it! Until then, there was no hot water to take a shower. That meant it was a matter of getting in, washing up, and getting out. No time for playing, singing, or dancing. My excitement about finally being in a home, and not in my car, or staying at a motel, helped a little to take my mind off the freezing water hitting my skin. I never had bills to pay before, and for that reason I was excited. I finally had somewhere that I could be for a long time. Having bills is a good thing like that, because no bills mean living on the street or depending on someone else. This time, I wasn't going to do anything that would jeopardize my blessing.

Just to be safe, I left the bill accounts in his dad's name. If I ever faced any hardship and wasn't able to pay them, then the payment history wouldn't be tracked back to me. I had never paid any type of house bills before. I didn't know how much all the bills would add up to at the end of the month. Just to be safe, I left the accounts alone without getting the name changed on them. The place was a mess. My first two weeks there, cleaning was all I did. I'd come home from work, play a Ne-Yo album that was saved on my Xbox console, and get to cleaning. I'm not a huge fan of him, but they were the only good songs that were saved on the first ever Xbox which I'd bought from someone a long time ago.

I started cleaning by throwing away the old junk that was never going to get used by me such as pots and pans. The stove was so disgusting. I wouldn't dare think about cooking on it. It didn't even work to begin with. Until I figured out how I was going to cook, I just ate out at fast food places. The trashcan outside would fill up quick. I tried to stack it up as high as I could without the trash spilling over into the yard or street. If only the trashman would have come twice instead of once a week, then I would have had that place cleaned up in no time. Neighbors across the street were looking on as I kept going back and forth dragging the trash out the house. I would clean until it was time for bed, then the next day I'd wake up, go to work, come back home and do it all over again.

At first it seemed like no matter how much I cleaned, the mess remained a never-ending cycle. After the trash can was filled to the top, I mopped the floors and got out the cobwebs that had built up in some corners of the home. Luckily, there weren't any spiders chilling there waiting to bite me. This was a job in itself, but it had to be done if I was going to call that house a home. I had a car and a whole house to myself. I never had a better feeling than I did then. The couch was my bed until I found the time to wash the bed sheets in the master bedroom. There was no washer or dryer.

The laundromat was where I was washing my clothes. Whenever my basket was full of dirty clothes, it was time to take them to be washed. This also was a good thing. It helped pass the time on weekends, instead of sitting in a house with nothing to do and just staring at the four walls. While my clothes were washing, there were always apartment or house magazines inside the laundromat to read. I would pick a couple up, browse through the different listings, and fantasize about living in one of the luxury apartments, or paying cash for one of those beautiful homes. Since everything seemed to be getting better, I felt as if it was only a matter of time before my fantasy became my reality. This also lit a fire in me to keep on pushing. I had come a long way from living out of my car to staying in a house that was paid for, but I still had a long way to go.

It took hours to get my laundry done. The dryer was the worst. It would take almost the same amount of money it took to wash my clothes to dry them. It was so slow. They must have had it rigged. It didn't matter which laundromat I went to; they had the same big bulky dryers that barely dry your clothes on the first go around. Since it was so big, I thought the heating element would dry my clothes immediately. While I was waiting for my clothes to get done, I would start with one housing magazine, then another, then another, then another, until I had looked at all of them. Weighing out my options is what I called it. It helped keep me feeling optimistic about the future.

One day, as I was in the middle of shopping for more cleaning supplies, I received a phone call from Tim.

"I'm going to sell the house. Three months of saving should get you back on your feet," he said.

Getting back on my feet in three months… how was that even possible when I was working on paying down the bills? Even if I did save up quite bit of money, it would go out the window being that getting a motel room would be my only option. There was nowhere else for me to go. If he was going to help out by getting me back on my feet, he needed to wait until I got an apartment. We got into a major argument over the phone, which we couldn't settle on good terms. He ended the conversation with,

"When I come over, we will talk more about it."

I was furious. I had a shopping cart full of cleaning supplies, and now I didn't know whether to put them back or keep them. I ended up buying them anyway. I figured it was going to be over a money thing, since it wasn't discussed in the beginning. If he wanted me to pay rent, that I could understand. I might not have minded doing that, depending on how much he asked for.

After weeks of cleaning the place, it was starting to look nice again… and just like that, the rug was swept right from underneath my tired feet. I didn't know for sure if he was going to stand on his word until we had the conversation face-to-face. He had stopped by from time to time, so I know he knew how hard I was working to get his dad's place comfortable enough for me to live in. All the old stuff that I was never going to use was out of the way, and I was replacing them with things that I was going to need. I also had a decent amount of food to eat throughout the week. I still wasn't buying anything to cook on the stove, just things to warm up in the microwave like hot pockets and pizza rolls.

The house was paid for, so me paying rent each month could earn him passive income. He didn't have to worry about a thing until something went wrong with the house, and perhaps that was the reason he didn't want the responsibility of keeping it. That weekend he came over and we discussed the issue. We settled on a reasonable amount that I could pay with confidence every month. *Guaranteed!* Then there was another deal added. If I took out a loan for him, then I could stay there rent free for three months. After that, I would have to make monthly payments. I was skeptical of taking one out, because it would mean paying back more money than what was borrowed due to high interest. He only wanted me to take out a little over $100 to live at the house for three months, rent free. I knew it was a good deal, but I wasn't going to keep doing it. We spoke back and forth about it. I made sure the deal was secure.

"This will be the first and last time I do this for the free three months."

"Okay."

I went to the loan office and signed the papers. Instead of my main priority being getting the bills down, it was the personal loan that had my attention now. I had to put a little bit on the bills to show them that I was making payments, but for my loan I couldn't do that. I needed to pay it off quickly, so I don't get behind on my other bills. Loans would cause my hair to turn gray in my mid 20s due to stress. Nope, not me. I needed to throw a lot of money at this debt to get it paid off sooner than expected. Everything seemed fine, but I had a feeling it wasn't going to always be like that.

There was a park that was near the house, within walking distance. I went there to play basketball. That's where most of the people hung out on the weekends. That was a big plus, because now I didn't have to drive anywhere and waste gas to relieve my boredom. During the week, there would be hardly anybody on the court. Most of the time, it was just me by myself getting my game tight for the weekend when the competition showed up. It still was in the hood, but there were no gunshots or people fighting over the game.

I visited my old neighborhood where I had to break into my on house in southside Nashville, and while I was driving around I spotted my old neighbor. We spoke and caught up on things. She knew how to braid, and I needed my hair done, so she agreed to do it at no charge. As we were talking, she told me a secret she had been keeping for a long time,

"You know… I always had a crush on you T-Mac. And still do."

"How am I supposed to have known that, Ashley? This is the longest we have ever talked."

She went on and on about getting together and hanging out, which I agreed to. I was "done" with Ladonna. I never did look at Ashley as ever being my girlfriend. I always thought she was cool, but not cool enough to date. She had a bit of a tomboy personality when we were younger, and always hung out with the boys but didn't dress like one. We immediately got intimate with one another. The only thing I regret about the time I spent with her was when I was teaching her how to drive. Love didn't even exist. *Periodt!* We had affection for each other, but without the relationship title. I guess you can call it friends with benefits, which we both were cool with.

I learned how to drive at the Tennessee State Fair Grounds when I was in my early teens, and made the same mistakes most people make. I had a foot on each pedal, but only knew how to control the gas pedal. That habit came from riding go-carts where it is required for you to have both feet on the pedals. My sister taught me to put my left foot behind my right. Doing that felt awkward at first, but the more I practiced, the more it became normal. My biggest trouble was keeping the car from swaying back and forth when going straight and making a perfect turn. The steering wheel would throw off my judgment because I didn't know how far my wheels would turn with each spin of the wheel.

At home, mom would park in the front of the house and let me drive the car around the block to park in the back. You had to go through an alleyway to get to the back of the house, and that's where I taught myself how to park backwards. Practicing by myself was better. Since I was always by myself when doing that, I could take my time and back up without rushing. The rear-view mirror was pointless. With my height, I got used to looking over the backseat and maneuvering the steering wheel while giving it the right amount of gas. Mom wasn't the best at teaching. She was impatient, and that made me overthink things a lot. Kiesha was calmer and more settled, and that's what made me think clearly. It took only a couple of weeks to get it down to where my mom could trust me to go up the street to the local grocery store to get something she forgot.

"And come right back." She'd say with a serious tone in her voice.

I would just have to learn the rules of the road, and that would come with more experience driving and studying. I passed both the written and driving test on the first try thanks to a cheat sheet. It was the driver's handbook that Michelle gave me, with all the highlighted answers that would be on the test.

One night, I thought it would be okay to teach Ashley how to drive. (Out of all the days we hung out, why did I choose to do it at night)? I took her down the backroads, where little to no cars ever traveled. I don't know why I chose to teach her on the road first, instead of at the park where most people have been taught. The road had very few streetlights, but it was enough to see what was coming up ahead. I took her around to show where she would travel, mapping out the course. Then it was her turn. She started off… bad. She didn't know how to put the car in drive! That was the first sign I should have paid attention to. I should've changed my mind there and then, but many of us didn't know how to put the car in drive our first time behind the wheel, right? She eased on the gas pedal, and we were off.

"Just take your time. No need to rush."

The first lap around, she did good. She got a little too comfortable, because she took her second lap faster.

"Okay, start to slow down a little, it's a sharp curve coming up."

The curve was approaching fast. She took her foot off the gas pedal.

"Put your foot on the brakes, but don't press down hard."

The car kept going the same speed.

"Are you pressing the brakes?!"

"Yeah!"

"Okay, press harder! *Slow down! Slow down!*"

We turned into the sharp curve and she panicked, losing control of the steering wheel. We ended up in the ditch. The car slid into it on its side. The hill was small, but had a deep slope. There was no chance of getting the car out. We were stuck.

"*Damn!* I told you to slow down!"

"I was... *I'm sorry.*"

We both had to crawl out the window. I couldn't believe what'd just happened. Then my instincts told me the only person I had to blame was myself. Teaching a new driver how to drive at night… yeah, not the best idea. Part of me ignored my instincts, the other part had sympathy.

"Damn mannn! Look at my shit!"

"You told me to slow down and I did."

"No you didn't! If I keep saying *slow down! slow down!* that means you not going slow enough!"

I didn't even have insurance on the car. The only thing on my mind was hoping that a tow truck could come out so late at night and get my car back on the road. After calling around, I got through to one, but he was a long way out. We would just have to sit in the dark until he arrived. My anger went out the window when she decided to make up for it. Yup, right there on the side of the road, in the middle of the night. No one was around, so it didn't feel uncomfortable. It was going to be awhile for the tow truck to get to us anyway, and this would be a wonderful way to kill the time.

"*Gulp, gulp, gulp...* T-Mac my jaws hurt."

"That ain't long enough… keep going."

"*Gulp, gulp, gulp.*"

After she got through, I managed to forget about the wreck even though I was staring at my car. It felt like a lucid dream.

When the tow truck arrived, they couldn't believe what they saw. It would be tricky to get it out because of the way it had landed on the slope. The way they were talking was like they were giving up before even trying. For a moment, they were looking to see where a good point to hook to was. He warned me that he could damage the bottom frame on the vehicle. I didn't care. How ever he got it done was fine by me. Time was steady ticking away. It was either tell them no, because of the possibility of frame damage, or get it out by any means necessary and hope for the best. They found a durable spot to hook to. He got in his truck,

"Y'all ready?" he said.

"Yeah."

He began to give it throttle. The car didn't budge. He kept giving it more and more throttle. Smoke was pouring out of his exhaust pipe. The power from the diesel engine cause it to roar. The car began to move, but it was scraping my gas tank on the edge of the concrete. *Screeeeeeeeeeech!* Ashley began to cry. She must have known that sound was a price that she couldn't afford.

"Stop! Stop! Stop!" his wife said.

He eased off the throttle. She told him what was happening.

"I'mma reposition the truck, cause it's not gonna work at this angle."

He got out and started looking around the car for another good spot to hook to. After he found a spot, he hooked up his latches and double checked to make sure that was the angle he wanted, inspecting every possibility.

"Okay, let's do it."

He got in his truck and began to give it another try. The throttle increased at a steady pace, as he was hanging out the window looking at his rear. Diesel smoke started to fill the air. The sound of the engine began to get louder. *Vroommmmm!* My car began to move, and the gas tank was scraping yet again. He eased off the throttle,

"Naw, keep going!" I said

He had momentum, and I didn't want him to lose it. There wasn't an easy way to get it out. It was all or nothing at this point.

The car began to crawl up the hill. The more it climbed, the more I had faith I would be home soon. As he kept going, the car kept moving till finally, it was free. Then it was a matter of if it would start back up or not. I put the key in the ignition and was a little bit nervous that it wouldn't start up. Then I took my time to turn it to the on position. After that, I quickly started up the car. It sputtered. sput, sput, sput, sput, Vroomm! "Thank you God!" They wanted to know what happened. As I told them, instantly they started laughing. I didn't mind that, and it was something I deserved. There wasn't enough cash in my pocket to pay him up front, so his wife rode with us to the ATM. I gave her the money and drove back. He left, leaving me with advice to never teach someone how to drive at night again. I thanked him and we went our separate ways.

"T-Mac, can I still go over your house?"

I paused for a moment, acting like I was unsure despite knowing damn well I still wanted her to. She was going to pay again for her mistake. What I had in store for her, she would need crutches when we were through. She knew I wanted to have sex, that was a rhetorical question.

"Mannn yeah."

When we got to my place, it was on and cracking. After taking her to "pound town," we fell asleep. When we woke up it was the finale of her punishment. It was time to leave her knees weak for weeks. After we wiped ourselves off, she needed to go home so I took her.

I had gotten comfortable living in the house. Cable was never going to be installed. That would just be an extra bill that I didn't need or want. I got my DVD player out of storage and had Mom's bootleg copies of DVDs, and that's how I entertained myself. It was this movie by Queen Latifah called: *The Last Holiday*, that inspired me. All her life she was playing it safe by staying in her little comfort bubble. Then she got hit with some shocking news that she would be dying soon due to a brain tumor. Her deep desire to do the things and go to the places she'd always wanted to go came to light. The inheritance that her mother left her, blessed her to live out her dreams. After she got over her sobbing, she realized the life she'd created in her *Possibilities Book* could come true. What else did she have left to lose?

That was a run-down house, and I was thinking way ahead in the future. I gave myself affirmations, "This is just temporary. My nice apartment or house is coming soon. That isn't a 2002 Maxima that I drive, it's a Lamborghini."

The Last Holiday is one of the movies that I love watching over and over. If you study the movie, like I always tend to do, it has an enormously powerful message: Live every day like it's your last.

In the morning at work on the construction jobsite, one of the cleaners came up to me while I was getting my tools,

"Hey, what is your name?"

"T-Mac Geezy."

"*T... Mac... Geeeezy*?"

"*Yeah.* You got it right. People always get it wrong on the first try, but you didn't. What's your name?"

"Samantha."

I finally knew what her name was, and could use it instead of referring to her as the girl with the big butt. She went on and on about how quiet I was. If she only knew where I've been and what I was going through, then she might understand just a little bit. I would spot her from time-to-time, cleaning or talking to someone. The blue jeans she used to wear made her butt look like it was imported from Brazil, or maybe it wasn't the jeans, maybe she got it from her momma. That thang was beautiful! And as a bonus, it was all natural and fitted her perfectly. Coke bottle shape, no cap. People couldn't help but to stop and stare at her "dump truck" as she passed by. Samantha was your typical southern belle, blonde hair and blue eyes, with a laid-back personality. Brittany was the get up and go one, always listening to music on her phone while jamming away. Both were two lovely individuals with a welcoming spirit that carried a country accent. As the days went on, I began to get more acquainted with them.

Samantha and Brittany forced me to be more talkative. Now, every time one of them walked past me, they stopped to have a conversation. I couldn't pretend like I was a wall and ignore them. They were too sweet. Then there were days they knew something wasn't right. They either waved and said hi, and in return, I would give them a small head nod. I could remember that some days even lifting my hand to wave back felt like a workout, and moving my lips to speak felt like they were stuck together. Around that time was when I would often go all day with saying less than ten words. I was comfortable not speaking at all, as if I were training to become a monk. How I communicate with people is by pointing, giving a thumbs up or thumbs down for varied reasons, or hum yes or no.

CHAPTER 14
WELCOME TO ATLANTIS!

It was that time of the month again. Time to make my car payment on my 2002 Nissan Maxima. It was this guy in the office that goes by the name, Hollywood. Why? I do not know. There was nothing flashy about him. He and the owner of the car lot were friends. Whenever he knew someone that was looking for a job, the owner would tell Hollywood. And whenever someone was looking for a car, Hollywood would tell the car lot owner. That was one of his spots to hang out. He told me about a job he worked at which he was one of the supervisors. They always needed help because people quit left and right. The job he was referring to was performing janitorial duties. He broke down what I would be doing day-in day-out, and what I was looking to make since I didn't have any experience in that area. It would be 3rd shift, so it wouldn't interfere with my daily schedule, and another source of income would benefit me more financially.

He made it seem like it was an obstacle course to get in. The receptionist was letting the people she knew talk to the hiring manager first. So, if you were someone looking for a job, (like me) and you didn't know anyone that worked there (also like me), your chances of getting in were slim to none. The story was that she used to have people go through all the time and trouble of filling out an application, and then shred it unless one of the higher ups saw the applicant in the room. He told me everything she was going to say.

The owner of the car lot told me it would be a clever idea. I was already looking for a way to earn more money anyway. My weekly check I had been getting was okay, but I needed to earn more money for the rainy days yet to come. And not only that, but it was also extra money to do simple things like take myself out to eat.

By Hollywood giving me the blueprint, I was able to go around obstacles that she had coming for me. I got to talk to the hiring manager and wound up getting the job. My schedule would be working on a night shift, part-time. Working two jobs wasn't new to me. I had done that back in college, which was worse, as I mentioned in my previous book, *Lost in My World.* Going to school while working at an electrical company full-time and a packaging enterprise part-time, was something. I figured wouldn't be a breeze. EZ Cleaning was only part-time, so it isn't like I would be sleep deprived.

On my first day, I already saw bad signs. The guy that was supposed to be helping me prep for cleaning was nowhere to be found. He would come and tell me what needed to be done, then disappear. We were the janitorial crew for the Grand Ole Opry. There was a lot of ground to cover in a short period of time, plus I wanted to make it back home to get at least a couple hours of sleep before it was time for me to head to my day job. I was part of the upstairs crew, but there also was a downstairs crew. There was a total of six people - three upstairs, three downstairs. We started off by picking up the trash, then mopping, after that it was vacuuming and double checking for missed spots. When we were cleaning, I noticed he would sometimes be gone for some time. That meant I was left with a lot of work to do by myself. I looked around in the auditorium and saw him talking to Hollywood, our boss, downstairs. I figured it was important, so I just focused on working. Minutes went by, and I saw them still talking, laughing, and joking. I would think Hollywood would tell him to get back to work, knowing other people were working and trying to get out as fast as they could. There wasn't a set schedule to come in. We just had to be done and out at a certain time, but those two were acting like we had all day. The other co-worker told me he always did that, every day they worked. I tried to play it cool by taking a break too. If he wasn't working, why should I? But then I remembered that I had another job to go to after that.

That job was probably his only one, so that's why he was trying to milk the clock. Not on my watch. I leaned over the railing,

"Hey I need some help up here!"

It was my first day, but I had to show him and whoever else that I wasn't going to pick up anybody else's slack. If you were in the building, then that meant you needed to work and help us finish on time. He gave me a look of disgrace. I didn't care. He got up and got back to work. At the end of the workday, Hollywood pulled me to the side,

"How did you like it on your first day?"

"It was okay."

"You made it clear he needed to get back to work, it was kind of my fault. He just likes to talk a lot."

"We had a lot of work to do up there and I needed help, so I had to say something."

My transition went well between leaving my night job and starting my day job. The extra money I knew that was coming in motivated me. The first week was fine, but the following week it started to wear me out not getting enough rest. I couldn't wait to leave my night job, just to rush home and get some sleep. Some days my plan would work out, then there were days when it didn't. Straight after work, I had to go to my next job to *try* and get some rest in the parking lot. It sucked, but it was something that had to be done.

No one knew that I was working two jobs. When I came into work on my day job, I felt like a walking zombie. I rarely ever spoke. But no one noticed. To them, that was my normal behavior. Something had to give, but my mind was so wrapped up in earning more money that I was putting my life in danger. In the times that we weren't busy, on either job, it was hard for me to stay awake. I would fall asleep standing up. My mindset was on my breaks, during which I would take a nap. Sometimes I would eat, then there were times that I'd rather sleep than eat. The only way my days would go smoothly was if they kept me busy and stayed out of my way. I would be so irritated at times due to getting such little rest. If there was a task that I could do by myself, I would gladly volunteer or just hop right in and do it. Whenever I was asked if I needed help, I declined. In some cases, help was needed, but I wanted to figure it out by myself because I like going at my own pace and being the lone wolf. There were times where help was needed and I had no other choice but to ask someone to assist me.

People on the job began to notice that Samantha and I were talking more. They could sense something was going on, but it was nothing really. We would talk about random things. It was weird to them that I liked the *Florida Georgia Line* music group,

"Baby you a song you make me wanna roll my window down and cruise."

When I said that line of the song, their faces lit up. When it comes to music, I like it all if it's good. They called themselves sisters. I thought they were saying that because they were best friends, and looked at each other as family. They were really blood related though. Samantha was the kind of girl I wanted. She was laid back and didn't require much to have a good time. Her age was well above mine and Brittany was a couple of years older than me.

Something Samantha never knew was that I always fantasized about being with her, just like most guys on the job. If my fantasy came true, she would be the first snow bunny that I had ever dated. And it'd also be my first time being with a country gal that had grown up in a completely opposite environment to the one I lived in. That was something interesting to talk about. I started to study her. Who she would always talk to? What were the subjects she loved to talk about? And lastly, was she single? She didn't wear a ring... but she still could have had a boyfriend. Judging by her looks, I could almost guarantee that she was taken. She seemed out of my league anyhow. Samantha and Brittany owned their own business, and I was working for someone. I'm pretty sure she had her own house, and I was back and forth living out of my car. Her pockets must have been full of cash, and mine were full of lint. I could tell she was older than me, but that's something I always looked for in a relationship. Her being older than me meant that she was wiser. God knows that I am a loose screw that needs tightening up from time-to-time! I tend to make stupid decisions that cost me a lot to settle. She could be someone to help me grow as a person. The girls I used to mess with were either the same age or younger than me. Everything that I could see was telling me that trying to get her to be my lady was never going to happen. I didn't insist on sending signals that I really wanted to get to know her on a personal level at first, but as time went on we talked more.

I hadn't seen my son since the last time I saw Ladonna, which had been months ago. Even though I had a place for him and I to sleep, my mind was all screwed up about taking care of my responsibilities as a father. I knew that by coming back around, my intentions would be to get back with Ladonna, and then the drama would resurface when I saw her and Mike together. I couldn't just be around my son without trying to get a sneak peak of how much her lifestyle had changed without me. Ashley would spend the night occasionally, but it was just a fling, nothing serious. We didn't know how long this fling would last, so we were just rolling with the punches.

After playing basketball at the park like I normally did, I went home to rest in the recliner chair. It was so peacefully quiet, just pure silence. Then I heard my phone ring. It was the supervisor that ran all the jobs for EZ Cleaning.

"Hey, you want to pick up some extra hours at another location during the day? The shift start at 5pm and wouldn't end till 8pm, with the *option* of working on a Sunday to stock up the toilet paper in the restrooms only."

I was already dealing with working a day shift full-time 6-3:30pm and night shift part-time. This would be a challenge to come in after my electrical job, then wait a hour and a half to clock in at the Cummins Station building from 5-8pm, then head over to the Grand Ole Opry. After that, it would be back to my electrical job. I wouldn't have time for myself, but I looked at it as a blessing. It felt better to be ahead on bills than earning barely enough to get by, so whenever the money called, I answered. After going over the hourly wage my answer was,

"Yes, I can do that."

There was not enough thought put into it when it came to the hectic schedule that I already was trying to maintain. Even though I had a tough schedule, more jobs equaled more hours, more hours equaled more money, and more money equaled less financial stress. If there was an opportunity to work at just one job and get paid more than the multiple jobs combined, of course I would *absolutely* sign up. But that hadn't happened yet, so I had to catch all the blessings God threw at me and trust the process that all of this would make sense later, but for now, I had to keep going.

At Cummins Station, we had to clean the men's and women's restrooms and some offices. It was an office building that had three floors. Me and another guy would clean the sink, mop the floors, fill up the toilet paper dispenser, and change the fragrance pads for the urinals. I never pictured myself as being a janitor, but it wasn't bad like I thought it'd be. I was thinking the restroom would be filthy, with piss and shit all over the floor, but that wasn't the case. Typically, we finished in a timeframe of two to three hours.

My work schedule was jam packed. I knew for certain that I couldn't keep it up for years and years to come. It was a means to an end, only temporary, but I wanted to go as long as my body would allow before it tapped out. Between Cummins Station and Grand Ole Opry, I much preferred work at Cummins Station. At least I could get home soon enough to get some shut eye from there, instead of sleeping in the parking lot at work waiting for the start of the shift to begin.

After working that busy schedule for a month, I had managed to get all the bills down to where I could take a hundred-dollar bill and pay the water, electric, and gas bill, and still get change back. I very seldom was at home, and whenever I left the house I unplugged everything to save electricity. The only two things that needed to be left plugged in were the refrigerator and the stove. Everything else—lamps, TV, DVD player, etc., was unplugged. Although it wouldn't cost that much to have those things plugged in, every penny counted to me. I was so happy that I had budgeted my money to get all the bills down to pay it like I had. Now that the gas was back on, I could enjoy hot showers. Everything was going well, except for my busy work schedule of having to fight to stay awake on my job and on the road. Then I was faced with another obstacle.

Tim called me. He wanted to borrow some money. The deal still hadn't been fulfilled yet about me staying there for three months rent free. Then, after that, I would start making monthly payments. I brought it up to him about our agreement,

"I don't care!" He said.

It wasn't a whole lot of money that he wanted, but a deal was a deal.

"I specifically told you that I wasn't going to give another dime until my three months was up."

In the back of my mind, I knew this was all too good to be true, but I tried not to dwell on the negative thoughts. I was living in the moment. He sense I wasn't going to let the agreement go.

"You need to get all my dad bills changed over to your name."

As I thought about it, it was me that needed to take care of my own responsibilities. When I would eventually get blessed with my own home, I couldn't put the bills in someone else's name. This is the real world. I was loving paying the bills in his dad's name, because at first I didn't know if I could manage paying all of them each month. If I had gotten behind on them, then it wouldn't affect my credit history because it was in someone else's name. But the truth was I needed to step all the way in and take this life thing head on. By me taking a hundred-dollar bill and paying all the bills while also getting change back, that showed me I had full control of my finances and that I didn't need to worry.

"I will change the name over."

I could sense where this was going. Once I agreed to that, there was another issue.

"You need to keep the grass cut low."

"How am I going to do that without a lawnmower? I don't know anybody who got one."

"Figure it out. Either keep the grass cut or move out."

I could pay a lawn care company to come and do it, but to me, that was a waste of money. The yard was less than half of an acre, and what they were going to charge me would not be worth it.

"Okay." *Click!*

Minutes later, I received another phone call. At first, I wasn't going to answer. I knew it wouldn't be good, but I gave in.

"*Hello.*"

"And I'm moving in."

But again, without giving him the satisfaction of getting angry, I remained cool.

"Okay."

I liked living by myself, but I looked at the positive side - that meant we could split the bills. When it came to me having company over, I knew that would be another issue, so I never told him about Ashley. When he moved in, I knew all of that would stop. He was going to have full control of the property and it'd be whatever he says, goes. Before that, there was guaranteed peace whenever I went home because it was only me in the house. I needed to look for somewhere else. My good life was starting to roll downhill and fast.

The only place I had to go was back to my car, or sleep at random spots and take quick wash-ups at convenience stores. If that's what I got to do, then I had to face it. Besides, it wouldn't be the first time I lived out of my car, but it would suck. Right when I had received my greatest breakthrough, there were thoughts that I would end up back where I didn't want to be.

The grass wasn't that high, so I still had time to come up with a plan to keep him off my back. My next-door neighbor always cut his grass. I figured I could ask to borrow his push mower to cut my yard. The only thing about that, he was Hispanic. I didn't know if he would understand my language, but even if he didn't, I could use hand gestures to explain what I was trying to say. If he wasn't going to lend me his mower and wanted to cut it himself, well then I would pay him if the price was reasonable. That wouldn't be an ongoing thing either. Eventually, I would find a way to do it myself. As we talked, he understood my English and agreed to let me borrow his mower.

Days later, Tim came by to check in when I wasn't there and saw the yard looking good. I knew he had been there because of the cigar he left. I had an issue with that. If he was treating me like a tenant, and he was the landlord, he couldn't just come in anytime he wanted and not give me notice. I was going to bring that up with him, but decided it would be pointless. If I didn't like it, there was the door, so I didn't bother saying anything.

Samantha hadn't been coming in to work lately, but Brittany had. Word got around that she'd hurt herself at work and had to take some time off to recuperate. I asked Brittany when she would be back. She didn't have an answer to my question, but gave me Samantha's number and told me she would be excited to hear from me. I didn't hesitate to call her when I got home to hear how she was doing. There was no answer, so I left a voicemail expressing my concerns. She didn't have my number, and so that was probably the reason she didn't answer. I don't blame her. Whenever I get calls from numbers not saved in my contacts, I typically don't answer either. I texted her to get an immediate response. Minutes went by without no reply. "Well, at least I'd showed that I cared." I was going to be respectful and not call her all the time of the day, or even unexpectedly. When I tried to reach out to her and she didn't answer, that was my first and last time doing it. I deleted her number, and the text I'd sent so I wouldn't "accidentally" try to contact her by phone. Me and Ashley hadn't been in touch for at least a month by that point. Maybe she'd moved on, maybe not. My focus was now on Samantha.

One time before she got hurt, I saw her run up to a guy and gave him a big hug. He wasn't even expecting it. "That muthafucka took my girl," I said to myself. "Why couldn't I be given the same treatment?" She was way out of my league. I couldn't take care of her like a man should. I was always on the move, working three jobs. I couldn't possibly find the time to hang out with her. Whenever I was not at work, I was in the house sleeping off my work schedule. The more I talked to her, the more interested she became. Then reality would strike when I spotted her talking to other guys on the job, being very friendly. It was like she was playing with my emotions, but it was my own thoughts that made it seem like she wanted to get to know me on a relationship level. My mind was playing tricks on me.

Hours went by before she responded through text message. She was doing better and would be at work soon. After reading that there was a smile that was permanently embedded on my face for a long time. I thought she wouldn't ever respond, but like her sister said, she was happy to hear from me and gave me thanks for caring. Right at that moment, I thought about when she would return to work… *I would have balloons, candy, and a teddy bear waiting for her.* Then I thought that would be too much for somebody I barely knew, and on top of that, her relationship status was still unknown.

The day came when I saw her and Brittany making their morning routines of getting their cleaning equipment. Excitement filled the room,

"Hey!" I said.

She acted like she was going to run up to me, then stopped and started smiling. I proceeded to walk towards her, and she did the same until we were face-to-face.

"*Hey!* Thank you for reaching out."

"No problem. I had to check on my buddy. Brittany gave me your number. I didn't know if it would be okay to contact you."

"It's okay."

We gave each other a hug and went about our business. I made sure my hug was nice, warm, and unforgettable. I didn't know the next time I would be that close to her again. It felt good to be embraced by her and take in the heavenly perfume that always lingered around her body. For the rest of the day, I thought about our hug and nothing else mattered.

The next time the grass needed cutting, I reached out to my neighbor again, but this time he wouldn't let me use his mower since it was his only one. If something happened to it while I was using it, it would be broken for months because I didn't have the funds to fix or replace it, so I understood.

I began to get frustrated when there was no one else that I knew who would let me borrow their mower. I was saving a little money, but I didn't want to spend it on getting the damn grass cut. On my night shift, I told Hollywood about my troubles. I didn't know if he had a mower or not. My intention wasn't to ask him if I could borrow one, it was just something that I needed to get off my chest. He listened and told me he had a weed eater that he would lend me. A mower was out of the question. Neither of us had the right vehicle to haul it, but the weed eater could fit inside of my car, and that was how my yard got cut, with a weed eater! It didn't take long to cut the front and the back. It was quicker than I thought. One thing was for sure, this wasn't going to last forever. I don't like to borrow things from people unless it is my only option. Being independent is something that was embedded in my brain since I was a young teenager.

Mom always told me, "Save your money. Stop spending it on candy."

Then, when I started doing that, it turned into,

"Why you always trying to spend my money? You got some. Spend your own."

When I turned into in adult, it became,

"You need to start figuring things out yourself. I'm not going to always be around." October 8, 2010, she died due to breast cancer."

I was hoping the grass wouldn't grow as fast, so it would be an easier task to control. Whenever I needed to cut my yard, Hollywood said I could use it anytime. That was nice of him, but I was not trying to haul around a weed eater in my car every two weeks whenever my grass needed cutting. Then I had to turn around and give it back to him the same day. I could've done it on the weekend, but that was usually when I wanted to be lazy and catch up on sleep. Just me in a peaceful, quiet house. I was still planning on being out of that house within a year. Me and Tim weren't going to see eye-to-eye.

After I got off work at Duewell Electric, I had an unexpected phone call. It was Samantha! I thought, game on. If she had a man, there's no way she would just randomly call me to chit-chat, but I still needed a definite answer.

"What are you doing?" she said.

"Nothing. I been wanting to ask you a question for a long time."

"Uh huh, what is it?"

"Are you single?"

"Yes," she said. "Are you?"

"*Of course*! I mean… yeah."

From that point on in the conversation, we started to understand both of each other's intentions. She had to get off the phone to take care of some business. I had to ask her one last important question that would put the icing on the cake. It was the temptation of staring at her butt whenever she was around that made me fantasize about her pulling this stunt. I never would've asked her in the past, but since she randomly called me out of the blue it brought our friendship to a whole new level. I texted her and was anxious to know what the answer would be,

ME: Do u no how to twerk?

It took her a moment to respond. I didn't feel that was an inappropriate question, but if it was, she would let me know.

SAMANTHA: Lol what is that?

ME: U no what it is. Why u txt lol?

SAMANTHA: Cause it sound finmy.

SAMANTHA: *Funny. My fone always txt random things.

ME: Can u pop yo booty?

SAMANTHA: Lol ummm noooo.

When we got on the phone that night, she asked me if I wanted to spend the night over at her friend's house. She would baby-sit the dogs when her friend goes out of town. It would be on a work night. I wanted to say, "Hell yeah!" but I needed to remain calm. "Sure," I said. I didn't want her to think I was excited about *potentially* getting some ass when it would be just fine chilling with her. I must admit, me getting some action would be a bonus. That woman had some cheeks on her, *good lawd!* I scheduled the night off from work. I couldn't pass up such a golden opportunity that had been presented to me.

Now that we'd started to become good friends, we didn't act like nothing was out of the ordinary when we were at work. I wasn't running around telling everyone that we'd talked on the phone. Out of everybody that seen her as an attractive woman, she had chosen me. I had brought my dreams into reality, and I didn't want it to fade away just because I couldn't keep my mouth shut. Whether or not anything would go down, it was still incredible to be taking in the fragrance that clung to her skin and clothes. I really loved her smell. It was only a couple of days until we'd spend some quality time together. The closer the date got, the more feelings I had that something would come up that meant she couldn't make it. The day prior to going, I had made sure we were still on with the plan when I saw her at work. She agreed and was excited for tomorrow to come. That's when I knew it was serious. Then a thought came to mind, *what about her sister being there*? We already were talking like there would be some action in the boom-boom room since there would be liquor, and tequila involved. Although neither one of us said anything about sex, I was curious about how it would all play out if we did get nasty. I'm pretty sure the house didn't have any soundproof rooms, so Brittany would hear her *screaming!* my name. When I got ahold of her, it would be hard for me to turn her loose. After work, I gave Samantha a call to see how we would manage to pull this off,

"Hello."

"You said Brittany was spending the night too, right?"

"Yeah, she's bringing a friend."

"Well, how is it going to work with her in the house with us?"

"Ohh trust me. This is a big house. *A mansion.* She will be on one end of the house, and we will be on the other."

The conversation ended when she explained it to where it made sense. I'd never been in a mansion before. I'd seen plenty that look like castles, and I didn't think she meant one of those, but I took her word that we could have our time and not be disturbed.

The next day, we had it all planned out. After work, I would go home to take a shower and dress nice since this was like a date. I waited on her to call me, since she got off later than I did, and packed some extra clothes to change into for work the following morning. A couple hours later, I received the text with the address that would lead me to that wonderful lady. I pulled up to the gate and entered, I could tell the house that she was in would be a big one.

"Your destination is on the left," my GPS said.

There she was, flagging me down to park in one of the four car garages. From the outside, it didn't look like much. Then I stepped in the house and it felt as if I should've been greeted with,

"Welcome to Atlantis!"

Inside were 4 bedrooms and 6.5 bathrooms, including a special bathroom for her friend's dogs. Yup, that is how the rich live I guess… with a special bathroom for her dogs. First off was a foyer with two giant doors for the front entrance, a game room, and a workout room upstairs. The upstairs was like an apartment. The bonus was a huge inground swimming pool, equipped with a diving board and separate hot tub!

I gave myself an exclusive tour of the place while she finished getting ready. This was my first time ever being in a mansion. I'd gone from sleeping in my car, to living at Tim's dad's house, to staying overnight in a mansion, all for free! Clearly, God was trying to tell me something,

"The best is yet to come."

I took it as a sign that my life was beginning to change for the better. Even though every time I felt that way, trouble would always make its way back into my life, I just couldn't help myself. It felt like a vacation being there. On top of that, she surprised me with a couple of music CDs.

After she got out of the shower and had on clothes, I picked her up. As she straddled her legs around my waist, I took my time savoring her kisses while my nostrils took in the sweet aroma of her body wash. My hands gripped her ass tight,

"Put me down, we have to save some for later."

"You right."

We went down to the kitchen to have ourselves a drink with Brittany. Her guy friend came over, and we all chilled for a bit before they took off to the night life. Samantha and I didn't want to go anywhere. We just wanted to stay at the house and enjoy our special time together. All my attention was on her, there were no distractions whatsoever. One characteristic that we immediately noticed in each other was that it didn't take much for us to have fun. We started off with a toast to the longevity of our friendship, with tequila shots.

Our conversations got deep. Secrets were shared with each other that we hadn't shared with anyone else. I felt comfortable telling her the whole truth about my situation, and it wasn't because of the alcohol. I asked her what her reason was for being so comfortable sharing such sensitive information with me, and she told me the same thing,

"The tequila is not the reason I'm telling you this. It's because I feel comfortable when I'm around you."

The moment was starting to get emotional, so I thought of a plan to make this night an unforgettable one.

"Let's jump into the pool."

"*Whattttt!?* It's freezing outside!"

"I know. That's what going to make it fun," I said, grinning with pure determination that I was going to get her to say yes.

"I think you had a little too much to drink."

"I feel fine. *C'mon,* it will be *funnnnn*. Have you ever jumped in a freezing pool before?"

"No!"

"I haven't either. Let's experience this moment together."

"Okay."

She ran and got some towels for us to dry off with. We walked outside and after she'd laid them down on one of the lounge chairs, she started running. Without any hesitation she dove straight into the ice-cold inground pool that was eight feet deep. There I was, thinking she was going to get to the edge and stop. Nope. She was courageous like me. That sent me into overdrive. I ran to the diving board, without any hesitation, jumped as far as I could into the water, and sank straight down. When my head reached the surface, the wind chills blew heavy across my face. We'd done it. We then only had to make it out of that pool before hypothermia kicked in. Once out, I rushed over to dry off before we went back into the mansion. She was just finishing up getting dried off. We were both shivering. We had survived jumping into the "Antarctic" pool.

"That was crazy! I can't believe I did something like that!" she said.

"It was fun right?"

"*Yeah*!"

"I told you. Let's do it again," I said, with a big smile on my face.

"Okay, but I'm not jumping in far this time. It will be a quick dip-in and dip-out."

"Cool."

She was the first to go again. I love to be spontaneous, so I ran to the diving board again and was going to do a front flip, but hesitated. I asked her to count down.

"3… 2… 1… *go!*"

I was running, then fear stopped me. I couldn't figure out why I was afraid to do a front flip. I'd done it plenty of times before in other pools. It took me two tries. On my third attempt, I succeeded. After we'd both dried off good enough, we took separate showers to wash all the chlorine off our bodies. We drank some more and wrapped up the night with our lustful temptation on empty. She was all I needed and wanted. We fell asleep together, with me spooning her.

My alarm woke me up the next morning. I was greeted with Brittany and her making homemade breakfast. It truly felt like a dream. She made me feel like a king. I ate what they prepared and headed to work. My shift started before theirs, which was good. By us coming in at different times, it would keep people from finding out what we had going on. I already knew they weren't going to tell a soul. I wasn't going to either. When we saw each other at work, we kept our cool and played it off like nothing out of the norm happened. It was our own little secret, and we kept it well. That is, until there came a time we had no other choice but to be noticed together. All tree of us.

I had invited Samantha over to my house (Tim's house really). I didn't think she would come, due to the fact it was in the hood. Little did I know, she'd grown up close to where I was staying. But she didn't know how much it'd changed since back then. There weren't as many crime scenes when she lived there. From what I'd experienced staying there, all the chaos was blocks and blocks away from me. She accepted the invitation. When that day came, she showed up looking good as usual with her high heel boots on. We turned on a movie and went straight to sex therapy. I wanted her to stay the night, but she had to leave.

CHAPTER 15
A NEW HORIZON

After two months of staying in the house, one night, I heard the doorknob jiggle. I had nothing to protect myself after having thrown away all of the knives when I first moved in when I started cleaning. I was helpless. It would stop, then start back up.

"Who is it!" I yelled.

No answer. The doorknob steady jiggled, like someone was trying to use a tool to get it open. It was around 10 p.m. I wasn't expecting anyone at that time of night. By that time everybody was usually at home, except for people who were out causing trouble. There was chatter, but I couldn't grasp who the voices were. Then the door swung open. It was Tim and his girlfriend. That pissed me off!

"You gotta call me when you about to come over!"

No response. They headed straight to the back. He was showing her around the place. That's when I heard the words that came out of his mouth that made my decision to move out for me.

"I can get this amount of money when I sell it."

He was still trying to sell it, even when we had a deal. I was going to pay rent every month. Now it was time to restructure my way of thinking back to being out on the streets, sleeping in my car. It will suck, but I did it once before, and I can do it again. That's what I told myself, reasoning it was better to live like that than to be stressed out on a place that I couldn't have true freedom in. There was no specific date, but I knew to be out before my months of living rent-free were up. I was going to keep my end of the deal, but if he was going to sell the house anyway, what was the point of me staying there trying to get comfortable?

In the very first weekend of November, I wasted no time getting my stuff out of there. I put most of my things in storage that I wanted to keep. The kitchenware I didn't take, because I wouldn't have any need for it. Then I was waiting on the right time to execute my plan to leave. I say plan… but really, there was no plan. Me waiting to leave was unnecessary. There was nothing on the other end waiting for me. Nothing except my passenger seat welcoming me back to sleep in. I'd already paid my storage fees and gotten the bills taken out of my name. The only thing that was left was for me to leave the house. I loved having the feeling of being in a house. Might sound funny, but I loved taking care of the responsibilities that came with it like paying bills. It made me feel as if my life wouldn't go back to where it had been.

The next time I met up with the girls at the mansion, I told both what was going down, and that I was back out on the streets.

"You can come and stay with us," Samantha said.

"Yeah, you will fit right in," Brittany added.

I really appreciated their kindness, but I wasn't sure if I wanted to make that move. It would be a life changer. I wanted to see if I could still somehow get a place of my own. I wasn't going to be sleeping in my car for long because I had people that cared for me, despite the fact they barely knew me. A while before then, I'd told myself that I wouldn't be spending that Christmas *alone.* Thanksgiving was coming around also. I figured spending Christmas by yourself is worse than spending Thanksgiving alone.

The first night back in my car was hard for me. I thought that it would be easy, since I had already experienced it. Going from paying your own bills at a house, to experiencing what living in a mansion feels like, it all seemed to be looking up. Well, that mountain climb had ended, and I had lost grip. The fall hit me like a bag of bricks. It felt like I'd accidentally hit the rewind button on my life. I had to play my cards how they were dealt and remain positive.

Famous quote, "Life is not all about being dealt a good hand, but playing a poor hand well."

I woke up in my car early one morning and Steve Harvey had left me words of encouragement. From what I remember he said was,

"Your current situation is not your future. There have been plenty of people with felonies on their record, who still manage to live a legit high dollar lifestyle. I was homeless for three years, sleeping out of my car. And now look at me. I have my own radio show and been in multiple movies. You have to keep the faith man."

That message was meant for me to hear. That pushed out most of the negative thinking. But some of it was still hard to overcome. I had thought that I was on the right path, only to find out it was a dead end. But life has challenges. That was something I knew all too well.

I didn't want to spend Thanksgiving around any family members. I was still torn. Samantha's family had invited me to come over to her gathering, but me with a whole bunch of country folk I didn't know? *No, no, no.* That would be too soon for my mind to take it all in at once. But I knew her family would be okay with it by how she explained it when she told them. At that point in my life, my body felt limp. I kept getting up just to get knocked back down. Kept imagining what my life could look like, then *bam!* reality always came up swinging. Somehow, I knew that everything was happening for a reason, and to trust the process. I was not thinking about suicide. I had tried too many times and *failed*, which was a great thing.

Thanksgiving wasn't a day that I felt like I needed to be around people. My first thought was to order pizza and chill in my motel room. My second thought was to go somewhere like a soul food joint and get a plate, since it would be similar to a Thanksgiving meal. But all those places were closed for the holiday. When I really gave it some thought, I figured being around different people would help take my mind off things. Golden Corral buffet came to mind, and that's the place I chose to go. It would have people around eating tasty food, and it would be affordable. I was all in. I took a shower, put on some decent clothes, and off I went. When I got there, the line was wrapped around the building. I was determined to tough it out. I wanted a holiday meal, and not something from a fast-food restaurant. The usual food that was made during these times is what I was craving; mac-n-cheese, chicken, green bean casserole, turkey dressing, etc. There wasn't anything that was about to stop me from having a good lunch by myself. I finally got a seat at a table. I hadn't eaten all morning, and was looking forward to that moment. My plate was stacked up, and when I returned to my table, I prayed over my food and began eating.

Everyone else around me had a table that was full of family and friends, and there I was by myself. The laughter, joking, and telling stories made them feel whole. I remained empty. No love was present, no one to sit and have a good 'ole time with. No one to tell stories with. That's when I begin to get choked up. I tried not to cry. It had seemed like all I needed was to be surrounded by food and people. And I thought that would help put my mind in the normal setting of being surrounded by family. As I looked at the chairs at my table and saw they were empty, that was when I decided being there was worse than staying in my room. Depression was manipulating my good emotions to let it in. I got some dessert, because I wanted to get my money's worth. After that, I left. I was there no more than an hour. I just wanted to feel normal again. When I got back to my room was when I gained control of myself. No one else could see that I was alone, and that was how I liked it.

My endurance ran out trying to juggle working three jobs. It had gotten too much for me to handle. One night, on our break at the Grand Ole Opry, all the crew members sat in the auditorium to wait for it to be over. I just needed to take a nap, the whole fifteen minutes. When I woke up, everyone was gone. I sat there for a moment, thinking they were going to come back. The time went so fast that I didn't even think that I had slept through the whole break. I finally looked at my watch and saw that an hour had passed.

"Oh shit!" I said, "why didn't nobody wake me up?!" I rushed upstairs where I had stopped cleaning, and that's when I saw one of my co-workers,

"Why y'all didn't wake me up?"

"The main boss here walked by, and we got back to work."

"Y'all still should have woken me up!"

"Hollywood wants you. He's over there."

I went to see what he wanted. Couldn't be good.

"Hollywood, you want me?"

"You got to leave now. You fired."

Without any argument, I left all my cleaning supplies right where they were and left. It was my own fault, so I couldn't be mad at him. It was only a matter of time before that happened on either of my jobs. And I was glad it had been that one because my body was more used to working days than nights anyway. The first time I decided to take a nap on break was the day I got fired. I still had the Cummins Station to do after my electrical job.

Samantha made it sound like I was going to get the comfort and love that I needed for the holiday, but it was too soon for me to be around strangers. They may have been her family, but they were not mine. If it was just her and her sister, then I would've loved that, but I wasn't going to ask them if they would spend time with me and abandon their family on a special day. If a miracle didn't happen quick before Christmas, then I would, without a doubt, celebrate it with their family. It was too hard for me to handle alone. I wanted to live somewhere that I didn't have to depend on anyone. A place I could call my own. My mind, heart, prayers, all went towards gambling and hoping that it would grant me the winning numbers to change my life forever. I was steadily blowing money, hoping that I could manifest that miracle. When the lottery numbers were drawn, it nearly always left me empty handed. When I did win something, it was just the lucky ball number… which was $2 at best.

Time was winding down on when I was going to move into Samantha's house and be "adopted" into her family. I gave her the date that would be my last day staying in the motel room, but I still had faith that I would somehow get my own place instead of moving in with her. That day never came. Samantha got dropped off by Brittany at my motel, so she could guide me to her house while I was driving. I got out all my bags of clothes I had and crammed them in my car. I left the other stuff in a storage unit until I was sure that was the place I would call home.

The drive was a long one down the same street, with no stops or turns. I kept thinking we'd missed our turn. Occasionally I would ask her, and her reply would be,

"Just keep going straight."

I knew she lived in the country. That would be a plus to be in a whole different environment. The whole ride, I was making sure that her kids would be okay with me there. They were old enough to understand that they would be sharing a home with a stranger. I had asked her what they thought about me moving in,

"The children love it. They wanted to see you on Thanksgiving, but you didn't come."

We went up and down and around all kinds of curvy roads before getting to her house. I pulled in the driveway and my nerves got the best of me. That was where I was going to stay, and it would help me out financially, but my nerves got the best of me. I had to get a buzz before I went in to meet the family.

"I'mma drop you off," I said, "I have to get a drank."

"What? I got some in the house."

"No, you don't. I'mma be right back. It won't take me long."

"I promise you I have some. It's left over from the first night you slept at the mansion. Come inside and I will show you."

I didn't believe her. I wanted to see if she was lying, and if she were, then I was going to go and satisfy myself properly. Not to get drunk, I just needed a buzz to calm my nerves. I got out of the car. Her daughter's dog, Misty, ran up to me,

"Man what the hell is wrong with that dog's eye?" I said, walking backwards.

"Hahahaha, I told you about Misty already."

It started to run towards me, so I hopped back in the car.

"Hahaha, she not gone bite. She just wants to sniff you."

The dog's eyeball was out of its socket. That's how bad the cat scratched it in the eye. Needless to say who the winner was in the fight. I let Misty have her way. She was a big dog, but not aggressive. She was going to have her way no matter what. I went into the house, and Samantha went to her cabinet and pulled out the tequila bottle. There was only two shots worth left.

"Can I drink all of it?"

"Yeah."

After licking the last drops off the lid, I had a slight buzz. That was good enough to calm my nerves. I stayed in her room. Her children came in to introduce themselves. It was her daughter that left a good feeling, like everything was going to be okay. She was talking to me like I wasn't a stranger. Like I had been there for some time and she knew me well. That made me feel welcome, but despite the buzz and the enjoyable conversation I was having with her, I still didn't feel completely relaxed. I thought to myself, *this is it. This will be my new place to live. My prayers have been answered. Now I know for sure I won't be alone for Christmas.*

My first day in, and already everyone was treating me like family. Then it was time to go to bed. I had been sitting in a chair that was in her room for the past hour.

"Get up here in the bed," Samantha said.

I wouldn't do it. The tequila had worn off, and I was back to being nervous again. I was waiting for her kids to be in bed before I got in. Her daughter, Judy, and her three sons came in the room to show off their dance moves. After the show, they asked me,

"Why are you still sitting in that chair?"

"Because I'm still watching TV." But really, I was waiting for them to go to bed.

They might have thought that I was crazy staying in that chair for so long. Eventually, I got in the bed. I still felt awkward seeing me in bed with their mom.

The next day was Saturday. Samantha had gone to work, and I was in the room by myself. Her daughter was the oldest and could take care of her brothers. I stayed in the room as long as I could go without eating. It must have been around 1p.m. before I checked the time. Then I heard a knock at the bedroom door. *Knock! Knock! Knock!* I ignored it. *Knock! Knock! Knock!* I figured that by this time, whoever it was, wasn't gonna give up.

"Who is it?"

"Judy. It some food in the refrigerator."

"Okay."

My stomach was empty and growling. I laid there for a few more minutes before getting up and going to the kitchen,

"You don't have to stay in bed all day. You can get up and fix you some food."

She was smart for her age, talking to me like I was the child. I laughed it off. They had plenty to eat, but I needed something to pop in the microwave and get back in my comfort zone with the door closed. A Hot Pocket would be quick to make, so I got two of them and ate in the room. After eating, I decided to go outside. Since I would be there for a while, I might as well get used to the surroundings. There was a trampoline outside. I went and jumped on it. It's been a long time since I'd been on one. I could do all the flips I used to do as a kid, back and front flips. That was what loosened me completely up, feeling like a kid again. Not caring what anybody thought or said. Shortly after, Samantha made it back home.

The property was amazing. It had a creek in the back, and I wanted her to show me around, so we went down there. Me and her talked about the past, when we were kids playing in the creek and getting all wet. Her creek wasn't full of water. We walked down it for a bit, then stopped. It kept going on and on and on. You couldn't see where it ended. After we got out, we went into the house, and she began cooking dinner. The last time I had a home cooked meal was when my mom was alive. "I can sure get used to this," I said.

The last holiday I spent with anyone in my family was with Keisha, back in 2012. It was now the year 2014. It seemed like it was a long time ago, but I'd become dull to not being around my real family. That didn't matter anymore. My new family was some good 'ole country white folks.

It was a couple weeks until Christmas. Everyone helped to put the tree together and decorate it. It has been a long time since I done something like that and it left me with this cozy feeling. As Judy was untangling the lights on the floor, a loud fart came out of nowhere.

"*Wow!* That was a big one," I said.

She didn't care. She just brushed it off and said,

"Here is the real me, breaking you in."

Everyone laughed. I didn't care. When you're with family, you're supposed to feel relaxed. Farts come free, so we can use them as much as we like. God had answered my prayers. I was putting together a Christmas tree with a group of people I called family. I'd told myself I wouldn't spend Christmas alone. And on top of that, it would be spent out in the country where I felt free and clear from my past.

All through the past months of being homeless, that type of feeling was what I was looking for but couldn't find. It was a big jump from that chapter in my life, but it was something that stood out that seemed strange. When I rode through the neighborhood, whether going home or leaving, people that would be in their yard would wave that didn't even know me. At first I thought that they must know someone with the same kind of car and were mistaking me for them. I had dark tints on my windows, so I brushed it off thinking they were waving at the wrong person. Then another person waved that I passed. *Don't they know that I am Black*? They had me confused. Usually, the people that wave at you know you in some way, but they didn't know me at all, and I am sure I hadn't seen them before. I rolled down my window at the next house that I passed so they would get a full glimpse of what I looked like. And again, they still waved. *This must be what people call southern hospitality*, I thought. These people aren't racist at all. It was an uneducated thought that was planted in my head when I was younger. My friend's uncle, who is Black, lived in the country, but he had a lot of land where no hatred could rob him of his joy, peace, and comfort. I thought the small country towns had a lot of racism, but I was proven wrong.

This was so different to the city life. In the city, people rush to go nowhere. And they do it with a lot of road rage. Such a change of pace would take some getting used to. My thoughts about the country were that everyone was racist and there would be confederate flags everywhere, with people shaming me for being Black. I didn't know exactly where Samantha lived, but I knew Brittany and her had their own business and, to me at least, they were rich. I didn't know anyone that was an entrepreneur. Before I'd actually seen both of their houses, I was thinking that they had big houses with a lot of land, living separate from everyone else. Samantha's house was okay. It seemed a bit too crowded at times, but it beat the hell out of sleeping in my car. Her house sat on an acre of land. A totally different picture than what I'd expected. Brittany stayed across the street from her.

One day, while all three of us were at work just chit-chatting, Brittany came up with an idea to go traveling somewhere. I hadn't been out of town in years, and it would be great. I didn't want to go somewhere that was close, I needed to travel to new heights. I'd never been on a plane at that time, so wherever we ended up, I wanted a plane to take us there. New experiences mean new memories, and I wanted to make some. The problem was, every place I chose were places they had already been, and everywhere they chose seemed boring. I wanted the vacation to be an extreme one. I was stuck on Island of Adventure and Universal Studios amusement park located in Florida. It would be worth the time and money with the different parks. They both had been there to Universal Studios, but not Island of Adventures. There had been new rides and other parks added since the last time they'd gone, decades ago. After about a week of them thinking about it, we were all locked in. Then we just had to come up with the money and pick the date. Spring was the best time. It was going to be the start of the season, which meant it wouldn't be crowded and the tickets would cost less. As soon as everyone got their money together, we were going to book our tickets and the room.

I was excited. Still, in the back of my mind, I was wary. Times like this would get me excited and then problems inevitably come to steal the joy that I had built up. Coming up with the money was nothing for me. I'd worked long shifts before and could do it again. Then I thought, if they backed out at the last minute would I still hop on the plane by myself? The answer to that was no. It wouldn't be as much fun. Then my son came to mind, if I were to take him then I couldn't live out the full experience. Some of the rides he wouldn't be tall enough for, and he certainly couldn't go into the bars, or nightclubs. I would just have to wait and hope for the best. In the meantime, I would need to put in overtime on my electrical job whenever they asked for volunteers for the weekend. I was already used to working all week long and saving up my money. The motivation would come easy for me, especially since this was an opportunity of a lifetime.

I spent a little money on Samantha kids to show my appreciation. My son spent the night with me on Christmas Eve to celebrate the big holiday in the morning. He also made some new friends. The kids took him in like he was no different as well. Life began to look up again. On Christmas Day, the house was filled with joy, fun, and a wonderful breakfast. It was such a blessing to be able to spend some time with my son in a setting that was comfortable and around people that were friendly. The biggest part was him opening presents with me, and then, going to his mom's house to open up more gifts. Sharing him on holidays was something we never argue about, because we both got to see him for a reasonable amount of time. Whoever he spent the morning with on that holiday had to drop him off at 10 a.m. with the other parent. Ladonna and I were getting on the same page about co-parenting.

CHAPTER 16
LIFE AMONGST THE WHITES

All through January, February, and March, things at home started to get better. And they stayed that way. It seemed like my roller coaster ride of highs and lows was over. I was just enjoying the constant upward direction and feeling like myself again. Samantha didn't make me pay rent because of my circumstances, but what I did in return was perform the general maintenance on her car like oil changes, change her breaks and rotors, etc., and help out around the house with things like electrical problems or even washing dishes. She saved a lot of money being with me. I gave her all the help she needed. Even when her radiator in her car blew, I paid to get it fixed with no hesitation. She asked me how much it cost, but I refused to tell her. I did it not to get any recognition for it, but out of the kindness of my heart. She was my girl. If she struggled, then it was my job to pick her up like she had done for me when I needed shelter and a family support system.

Her mom lived next door to her. I always wanted to go over there to introduce myself so she could properly meet me, but I was nervous. Samantha told me a story about when she was younger how her mother wouldn't allow any of her children to date Black men or women. Being friends with the Black people wasn't a problem. She wasn't racist, far from it, but because of the word of God, "Stick with your own kind." Samantha and I both agreed on the same thought. What we took it as was to stick with your own religion which race didn't play a factor in. Christian believers stick together, Muslim believers stick together, and so on. Samantha had married a Black man before, and I guess he finally broke the ice. Her mom had already heard of me prior to me moving up there.

I would build up courage to go over there, then get stopped in my tracks. I would see her sometimes looking out the screen door, enjoying nature's beauty, but she never saw me. Then came the day that I finally did it. I walked in, went straight to the kitchen where she was, and introduced myself. Her home had a peaceful, welcoming spirit to it. I gave her a hug, and it felt good. It was a feeling that I don't get too often.

"Mom, where are the pictures you have of the family when we were younger? I want to show Terrance."

"They're in my closet. Be right back."

I was a little bitch. Only way I was going to go over there was if Samantha came with me. She played a big part of keeping the conversation going. Looking at pictures of Samantha, I saw that not much changed… except for her amazing body of course. It felt good to know her mom. I grew up without a grandma, now I could experience that feeling. The kids were always calling her granny 24/7. "Granny, granny, granny," they would say, so I became accustomed to doing it myself. It may sound strange for me to call her granny instead of Mom, or Ms. Mitchell, but calling her granny felt more comfortable. Even her own daughter used to call her that sometimes. I started to go over there more often, without Samantha, to spend some one-on-one time with her. Every single time I walked in her home, I became filled with this welcoming spirit. I wasn't a little bitch anymore about going over there by myself.

The time had come for us to buy our tickets to Disney World. The only people going would be me, Samantha, Brittany, and Brittany's friend. We started searching for our tickets and looking up information to help us stay away from fake websites that scammed people, but we also wanted to get a cheap deal by going through a third-party website. Eventually, we ended up buying the tickets off the official site. We felt more secure, and even got to save money when we bundled the parks together. Samantha and I picked a different hotel than Brittany and her friend. We settled for a three day stay. Our tickets had the bundle package of Universal Studios, Islands of Adventures, water park and we purchased separately the City Walk, where you can go into different clubs free of charge! With everything included—round trip on the plane, hotel, and park tickets—it wound up costing no more than $800, for Samantha and I combined. She was going to pay for the rental car and gas. I was thinking about upgrading to first class seats, since I wanted it to be the best time ever in life, but I was quickly reminded not to do that. My budget was tight after I checked my bank account!

After thoroughly checking everything ten times, I submitted the payment. We were locked in for good. The trip was set. "Orlando, Florida. Here we come!" We all started acting crazy. It was my first time being on a plane, and it was a huge deal for me. I always loved heights. To be 10,000 feet in the air for the first time, meant I could officially say my life had reached a new chapter.

That year was when I enrolled in apprenticeship school to become a certified electrician. They put me in a second-year class. Everything they were talking about were things I already knew from tech college. I didn't think about me being in the second-year class until I met someone who went to the same college, had the same class, and graduated on the same day as me, but he started off in his third year instead of his second. I couldn't figure out why they put him in the correct year but were holding me back. The credits were transferable, and everything should have fallen into place without a problem. He told me that they tried to do the same thing to him and that, after he did some research, it turned out that the college only gave a few people every credit they earned. The only way it would get fixed was if I called the tech college and told them my issue.

Them fixing my credits in the database wasn't a problem anymore. The only issue that I had was the apprenticeship school giving me a hard time after my credits hadn't been updated in the system. But I had proof. The president, Mr. Bailey, at Duewell Electric was also one of the board members at the school. I thought it would be a quick correction after talking to him. He could show the facts to the other board members, and that would be enough to change my year. Only in a perfect world. We went back and forth, week after week. I started out by calling him, but then I started to pop up right after work to have a face-to-face conversation. He told me he would talk it over with the guys, but every time I came to the office and brought it up he would say, "We're working on it." He showed me the old transcript. The one with the credits issue. I was prepared for that, so I brought the updated transcript that proved I passed my first and second year lessons and belong in the third of the electrical apprenticeship program. There was no acknowledgement given. He probably thought I typed it up myself. I insisted that he check online, in the national database so he can be sure. “There is not enough time for it,” he said. It was something that would take no more than three minutes to look over, and he didn’t have time to do it… yeah, that was a red flag.

I felt like I wasn’t getting nowhere with him. The next step was going to talk to the director of the school, Joe, to help me out. Joe had an office in the school. I felt like I could get the info moved quickly since he ran the school. Rumors went around that he was difficult to get along with. Fine. I wasn’t trying to become friends with the man, I just wanted to be put in the right year, without any discrepancies. That was it.

After I met up with him and showed proof that I was in the wrong year, “I will see what I can do,” he said. He will see what he can do? I mentioned about me talking it over with Mr. Bailey, wanting to know if he got the memo,

“I remember hearing something about that, but I haven’t looked into it.”

That was why it was taking so long. I did my part by talking to the main guys, now it was their part to deliver me the good news. I had been in school for a month. Each week that passed meant more work to make-up to get on track with everybody else when I did get put in the third year. The many tests and mountain of homework that I would have to do was weighing heavy on me. Why couldn’t they just do their job so I could be successful down the road?

I built up so much stress that I blew up the next time I met Joe. I was done talking to Mr. Bailey. It had gotten so bad that I told both of them that I would start to record our conversations every time we spoke, for understanding purposes. Joe would say one thing, and Mr. Bailey another. The only way to make it happen would be through Joe. He was the director of the school. So, then came the day that I went into his office with my phone already recording.

“Hey, Mr. McAdoo.”

"What up. Here is everything you need to put me in my right year."

"Why are you stepping over your boss's head? Didn't he tell you he would get back with you?"

"I talked with him multiple times. You are the only person that can correct the mistake since you are the director."

"I told you we are working on it."

"It's been a whole month now. What's taking so long?"

On and on we went like that, back and forth till the anger let itself free from my inner thoughts. I ended the conversation by telling him that I would go to whoever that was over his position and tell them what's going on. He laughed it off as if I were joking. I wasn't and called that person and left a voicemail.

The next day, Joe must have told Mr. Bailey about our intense argument. Mr. Bailey called me while I was at work and told me that I needed to meet with him after I got off. I didn't care if I was about to get fired. There were plenty more electrical jobs out there. Not all of them pay for your schooling like Duewell Electric did, but I was determined to find the right company that would offer that benefit. It was irking me beyond belief how they were beating around the bush. The same procedure they had followed to put me in second year should be the same procedure they could follow to put me in my third. There was no reason for it to go on for this long. I knew they probably had meetings and other things to do, but c'mon! A full month of, "We're working on it," was unacceptable. After work, I went into Mr. Bailey's office clear minded and ready for anything.

"Sorry that it took so long. Here is the paper that you need. Just give it to the lady at the front desk of the school and she will give you your new books after you turn in the old ones."

I kept calm, not buying into his sympathy.

"Thank you," I said, grabbed the paper and left.

Now it was a matter of figuring out how many tests I had to make-up. The headache of going back and forth was over for good. I officially was in my right year. I handed the paper to the lady and exchanged my books. As she handed each book to me, one-by-one, I made sure each and every one of them were for 3rd year. I was ready for any flaw that came up. As I walked into the class, I saw Joe standing there talking to my teacher. I sat at the front of the class, because all the seats in the back were already taken. As I was walking to my desk, he spoke,

"Hello."

I was ignoring him, still feeling deep fucking resentment about him making it so complicated when the only thing I was trying to do was get some help.

"Hello," he said again.

That's when I tucked in my pride and spoke.

"What's up."

He could tell I was still angry about the whole situation. I didn't want to acknowledge that he was speaking to me, but I was finally in the right class and now that whole ordeal was in the past. He walked out of the class shortly after I sat down.

Now it was sink or swim. I had to make up three tests to get caught up with the rest of the class. It was extremely hard, because during class I had to pay attention to the lesson the teacher were currently talking about, then study for the previous tests at home. I was so anxious to get caught up that I studied for only a day for the first test and the results showed as much. *Failed.* The good part about it is that he would give your test back so you could see which answers you got wrong. The test would be in the same order the following time, with the same questions, so I studied the ones that I'd gotten wrong. The second go around was a success. I passed the other two tests on my first attempts. Those two weren't as hard as the first one. So I was all caught back up then, and I could breathe better.

The teacher, Mr. Brent, was an experienced electrician. Just what the class needed, not some random person who knew nothing about the electrical field except for what's in the book. He'd been on many jobs, and encountered many problems that we might one day face. The stories that he told us were ones we could all relate to. Some of the information in the book we would never need, like calculating voltage drop. On the job, the engineer has the calculations already on the blueprint. But it was still a good thing to learn, just in case we wound up doing side work and needed to figure things out like how many plugs can go on a 15-amp breaker. A couple of people that were in my class at Miller-Motte were in that class. Everyone in there was working for an electrical company that paid for their schooling. If we passed all our classes, we didn't have to pay a penny out of pocket. The company took out $50 every paycheck for schooling. That was a way to keep us in check because if we failed for that year the company kept every penny, and you will have to retake that whole year. You must pass every year with at least a "C" average.

Florida was one day away. I only worked a half-day at Duewell Electric. There were still errands I had to run like getting my hair braided and buying fireworks. It was going to be a light day at Cummins Station, and I had planned it out ahead of time. I would come in, quickly do my thang, then bounce. Once I had arrived at the job, I couldn't get into the building without someone using their key card or opening the door from the inside. I called my coworker twice, wishing, hoping, and praying he would answer. He didn't. After ten minutes of waiting, *zoom!* I was out of there. A couple minutes later, he returned my call,

"Hello."

"I got your missed call. What's up?" he said.

"I called you because I couldn't get in the door."

"Okay, I'm heading downstairs now."

"I already left now. I got a lot of stuff to do to get ready for my vacation."

"Cool, see ya later."

"Aight then."

And that was the end of the conversation, without any arguing about someone picking up my slack. That day was perfect to skip. My duties would have taken me two hours to complete, and that's if I went at turtle speed. I honestly could have been done within an hour.

I got to the beauty salon at the right time. It's usually packed, but luck was on my side. I wanted it to be a quick job. Get in and get out. I got braids, straight to the back. Next stop, fireworks. It would be a night to remember for everyone. I spent over $200. I mean come on! This was Florida we were talking about. I would never know when I would be able to have an opportunity to go again.

The sun beat me home. I wanted to set up all the fireworks in a sequence, but couldn't see nothing outside. This is the country. Ain't no streetlights out there. Using the flashlight on my phone, I began looking through my bag to see what I was going to pop first. All the kids and family started to come out. Everyone except granny. I'm guessing it was her bedtime. I thought about a drumroll, so I started out with everyone counting down. Then I lit up the full belt of black cats, over one hundred of them. It was time to celebrate! 5…4…3…2…1 there was a brief silence… then *pop-tat-dat-dat-pop-tat-dat-tat-tat-pop-pop-pop!* On and on it went. Then the big cake boxes, *Boom-Boom-Boom!!!* After that, it was mortar time, I lit the long wick of the firework *sssssssssssssssssssssss Boommmm…Poowwww!!!*

We were all having a fun time until one of the smaller fireworks landed in our neighbor's yard. From what I knew, Samantha's family always had issues with them. There was chatter back and forth. Then I heard her something most Black people don't like to hear,

"I'm calling the cops!" the neighbor yelled.

Samantha yelled back,

"Tell 'em, come on!"

Noooooo, what was she doing? A cop seeing a Black man with a whole bunch of white folks in the country. I thought smart in that situation. I didn't want to stop, because I still had plenty more fireworks to pop, so I continued. I lit one and moved to the next one. Light and move, light and move. The police showed up fast. Another cop arrived minutes behind the first. We could see him driving up to the neighbor's house. I stayed outside as long as I could. Once they left the neighbors and started to come toward us, was when I got my ass in the house and peeped through the blinds. I didn't have any warrants, my fear was based on the world's—and not my own understanding. Not all cops are bad, but still, with everything going on these days you better take precautions.

Two big, country fed white police officers stepped out of their cars and started talking to the family. I stayed in the house until everything was settled, and the cops were clear out of sight. I didn't want any part of that, even though I was the one who *accidentally* caused it to go over there in her yard. My family had my back. They knew I did it. They saw me do it, but they knew it was an accident. Samantha had explained the reason for all the fireworks, but not once add my name in it. The cops understood, and just like that, the show could continue until 10 p.m. We were going to be done before that time anyway. I still lit the fireworks, but not the ones that had wings. You can't ever tell which direction they're going to fly in.

When the show was over, we cleaned up and only had a couple of hours to sleep. I had set the alarm on my clock and my wristwatch to get up on time. There was a checklist prepared for all my clothes and things to make sure I had everything.

Brittany was going to spend the first day with us, until her friend arrived the following day. We needed to be at the airport two hours early in case the lines were long. Before I went to sleep, I checked to see what the weather was going to be like. Our first two days looked like they were going to be good, all sunshine, but our last day called for 100% chance of rain. Only thing I could do was pray and hope it didn't ruin our vacation of a lifetime, even though it would be on our last day. Brittany, Samantha, and I got dropped off at the airport by their sister. They gave me the run-down of everything I needed to do to make our check-in at the airport go smoothly like wearing slippers, because they are easy to take off and put back on. And have your belt off, and keep your jewelry, wallet, and phone in hands before getting to the metal detector.

It was my second time ever in an airport, but it seemed like my first. While we were waiting for our plane to depart, which was still over an hour away, me and Samantha got something to eat. The sun began to rise. Despite the little time we had to rest, our minds were filled with excitement that overcame the tiredness. They had gotten coffee to give them an extra boost of energy. I couldn't drink coffee if it was the only thing left to drink on earth. That shit is nasty.

One day, while working at Dunkin' Donuts years ago, I decided to try and give coffee a shot. Though I'd tried it before when I was younger and not liked it, I figured it probably would taste better if I fixed it up myself. I poured my coffee and added cream and sugar to it and tried it. I could still taste the bitterness, so I added a boat load of sugar. The after taste was gone. All the sugar I added for it to fit my taste buds isn't going to be good for my health down the road. Hot coffee or cold coffee all tastes the same to me. Bad. Many people are addicted, and would be late for work so they can have their mocha cappuccino. Some just desire the taste, and others can't go on without the turbo shot that can be added to it. I figure if I wake up in the mornings tired, then that's a sign I need to go to bed earlier. That's one of the ways that I discipline myself. Go to bed early, wake up feeling refreshed. Go to bed late, you must suffer the consequences in the morning. I will never try coffee again unless they somehow make it taste like candy. That should be a recipe in the future.

Our time had come to get on the plane. I called first bid on the seat by the window. Now that we were all buckled up, our flight took forever to leave with the attendant going over safety procedures.

In my mind I was like, *look lady, if this plane somehow goes down, we are all gonna die. Little masks and emergency doors don't mean a thing. Let's get this plane moving! The amusement parks is calling my name!*

The plane started to head towards the runway. My adrenaline was pumping because I knew what was about to come next, high speed for take-off! The plane lined up with the runway and stopped. "Oh boy, here we go!" Seconds went by, then minutes. "Damn, what is they doing?" Moments later, I could hear the engines firing up. It grew louder and louder and the plane started to slowly move. I was recording with my phone. I couldn't help but smile hard showing all thirty-two teeth.

The speed gradually increased and then, we had lift off. It felt like I was leaving the old life behind and heading towards a new journey. The kind of journey everyone would love to take where you can laugh, play, and create good memories. I would have loved to be in the sky during sunrise, but it had already been hours since then. The flight attendant came by with a choice of plain Lay's potato chips or pretzels. I was looking for the chicken dinner as seen on the TV shows and commercials. Samantha told me not to hold my breath. What you see is what you get, and what I got was some plain chips, and a couple of alcoholic drinks. Me and Jack Daniels were going to be relaxed on this trip. Plus, everything was free, so there was no room for complaining. It was now time to sit back and enjoy the flight.

It took us two hours to reach our destination, but it seemed longer due to the adrenaline rush of wanting to be there in minutes.

"This is the captain speaking, we have now arrived in Orlando, Florida."

The airport was huge! I thought all the airports were the same, but this one took it to a whole other level compared to Nashville's. From the charming floors you walk on to the glamorous artifacts that were displayed all around, it was a dream for me. On top of that, there were palm trees in the airport, along with a hotel. The airport was so big that we had to take the shuttle train to take us to the other side to get our bags. I'd never been on a train in my life! Everything was starting to look like a new world to me. After everyone got their bags, we took a shuttle to our hotel and the driver gave us all kinds of information about the beautiful city.

We all agreed to do the water park first, since the sun was showing its beauty with no clouds covering it. After that, then do the rollercoasters later. We made it to the hotel before it was time to check-in. Forget waiting for our room to be clear, we put our bags in the storage closet where we knew they would be safe, put on our swimsuits, and headed right back out to have the time of our lives. The hotel Samantha and I were staying in was within walking distance of the water park. We saved a couple of dollars by not calling for an Uber. Everything went smoothly. I was sure that the lines would be wrapped around the parking lot, but that wasn't the case. We didn't have to wait that long. Only a few minutes went by before we entered the Water Kingdom. The only water parks I'd been to before then were Wave Country and Nashville Shores, but they were kiddie parks compared to Orlando's! There were gigantic water slides everywhere! If you know me, then you know I like to get my money's worth. If it was for free, or a ride that I had already paid for by purchasing the park ticket, I was going to be on it. I even had to have the experience of being at a kiddie area where it looks like a jungle gym when entering. Waterspouts were everywhere, but the best part was waiting until this big bucket got filled. Once the water reached the top, it caused the bucket to tilt over leaving you drenched at the end. I would not let a single dollar of my ticket price go to waste. I didn't know when or if this would happen again, so I was determined to take advantage of every single moment.

All of us started off in a group. Then Brittany wanted to lay out to get her skin bronzed from the sun after she went on all the big slides. Samantha was on my level of excitement. There was no time to sunbathe when there were such wonderful, exciting things right in front of our faces. We let her be and continued our quest. Brittany loved the sun, and there's nothing wrong with that, but again, I had to get my money's worth. This moment would leave us with the curiosity of what more Orlando had to offer that would leave a stamp on our memories we would never forget.

A couple hours later, I received a text that our room was ready. There was still more to do though. I didn't want to go all the way back to the hotel just to put our bags away, only to come back and finish what we'd started. That would be wasting too much time. There was nothing to worry about. Our bags were safe, and we had our money on us, so we stayed until our pleasure was fulfilled.

As the sizzling heat started to cool down, we got our stuff together and headed to my room. We had been ripping and running all day, non-stop. Before we got in the room, we could see off in the distance The Sling Shot ride. On that ride, you get into a capsule and it lowers you down. The level of expectation intensifies as you wait to be released and shot up in the air at extreme speeds. Once you reach the peak, it bounces you up and down until it settles. I always wanted to do it, but it wasn't in the budget plan. Samantha and I still agreed that we were going to try it while we were down there. You only live once, right? And I'm an adrenaline junky when it comes to heights. I set my alarm clock to wake us up on time to have a delicious continental breakfast. After that, we would catch the shuttle to the parks.

Beep! Beep! Beep! Beep! Beep! Just when I was finally getting into a deep state of sleep. I didn't want to move. It seemed like I had been tossing and turning all night thinking about the next day. When I finally went to bed, it was only a few hours before I had to wake up. All the excitement of thinking about the roller coaster rides kept me from getting a comfortable night's sleep. The temperature in the room was perfect underneath those fluffy white blankets, but I had to put my two feet on the ground and get the day started. The bacon, eggs, sausage, and biscuits had my mouth watering just thinking about it.

We had managed to find a table all three of us could sit at. After eating, I filled out the lottery slips—Mega Millions and Powerball—to hopefully win it big while in Florida. Our shuttle wasn't arriving anytime soon, so I had time to concentrate on what would be the next lucky numbers. I asked them for some numbers to pick while also picking my own. With all three of our brains put together, it was possible that we could win the big prize. I thought about what I would do if I did win it big while on vacation. I would *definitely* extend our trip. Then after that, it would be all about handling my responsibilities as a man, making sure all my necessities were taken care of and spreading the riches around through my generosity of giving.

Moments after filling out the whole two slips, our shuttle came to pick everyone up to go to the parks. When we got there, we had two options: Islands of Adventure or Universal Studios. As we looked at the map, we made a vote of which park we thought was going to be the one that knocked our socks off the most. Since we were only going to be in town for three more days, we picked Islands of Adventure to do first, since it had more exciting rides. The following day, we would go to Universal Studios, then our last day would be spent back at Islands of Adventure.

It was at least thirty minutes before the park opened, and the entry lines were already packed and people were getting impatient. There was no sitting down for us. I knew if we wanted to get to enjoy ourselves without waiting in long lines, we needed to be standing up front and knowing which ride we would hop on first. That was *Harry Potter*. At first, we thought that ride wasn't going to be that exciting, until we asked around to see which ride was the best. It came down to Harry Potter, so we mapped out our route, using the park map, and were ready to get after it.

"Okay everyone, the park is now open! Enjoy!"

As soon as the gate was released, everyone ran to where they wanted to go. That was the funniest thing. It looked like the starting line of a marathon as people rushed in.

My bunch was the first to get on the ride. We sat down and got strapped in properly. "Okay now, *enjoy,*" the ride attendant said. Curiosity filled our minds about what was to come. Right off the bat, it got interesting. We were flying on the simulation screen with the wind blowing in our faces. It was the realest feeling you will ever feel on a simulation ride. It wasn't just a screen put in front of us, the seats actually moved to different scenes. It was like a simulation/roller coaster combined. When our ride finished, there wasn't anyone waiting.

"We have to do that again!" I said.

"Yeah! Excuse me sir, can we just stay on? We want to ride again," Brittany asked.

"Sure. I just have to make sure everything is still working properly with the safety arms," he said, as he went through the procedures again of locking us in.

"Okay, y'all are good now. Have fun."

"Ohhhh shit! Here we go! Ahhhhhhhhh!" I said.

I looked to my right and saw Samantha. She was dialed in, eyes buck wide open, wearing a McDonald's smile. She was ready.

We still wanted to do it again after it was over, but people were in line waiting by that time, so we had to get off and go back through the line. There still weren't that many people though. It was only seconds before we were right back at our peak level of adrenaline. That ride was crazy! There still was a lot more park to cover and so after the third time, that was it. Brittany met up with her friend. We all agreed to meet up later to have fun and see what the late night Florida vibes felt like. So then it was just Samantha and me. I think the reason me and her clicked so well was because we both have similarities when it comes to getting our money's worth. Money didn't come easy in our line of work.

The next exciting ride we got on was called, *The Incredible Hulk.* It starts you off slow, then halfway up the roller coaster it shoots you off, unexpectedly, like a bullet! You couldn't help but scream. It is non-stop speed. We got on that twice, even though the lines were super long. It was worth the wait. The smooth steel that the roller coaster rides on lets you enjoy every moment of it, unlike the wooden rides that shake your body from beginning to end. Those were still fun to me, but they sure beat you up.

We went to every ride. And when I say every ride, I mean *every ride.* After walking for hours, we decided to get on the kiddie coasters to relax our feet. She was struggling to keep up while I was still in full stride. Dr. Suess was one of the rides we got on. There were no restrictions for us riding it, so we buckled up and chilled out. There were even palm trees that made it look just like pictures in the books. You know those tall trees that are curved in different directions? The parked nailed those. As we cruised along at a snail's pace, we began to think about where to go next. They had shows that people performed in at specific times. We managed to catch most of them, and planned to catch the ones we missed on our last day.

As the sun began to wind down, the nightlife began to glow. Neon lights lit up the walkway. We had to leave to catch the shuttle back to our room to get ready to leave our mark on Florida's nightlife, but first, we had to experience the *SlingShot Ride.* It was within walking distance of our room. We got there in no time. We didn't know there was an arcade attached to it. Temptation filled the room. There were all kinds of games everywhere inside, and outside were go-karts. I remained focused on what I came for. We got our tickets and hopped right in the capsule. She is not a fan of heights, but she loved to experience new things which I thought was cool because I didn't want to be alone. We got locked in our seats, and there was a camera rolling to catch every facial expression. We were lowered and then waited patiently. Right when we got relaxed, *Whoosh!* The latches released. We lifted off. The G-force kept building stronger, the wind was howling in our ears, we reached peak altitude in no time. It was fun, but what the ride attendant expected was not there. He knew I would be cool, since I was excited to get on in the first place, but Samantha was freaking out as we entered. He thought she would make a funny face from being so damn scared, but she remained calm during the whole thing. After being at the park all day, it was more like a sit and chill ride. It was still fun and exciting. When we got off, he showed us the video of our facial expressions. There was nothing but big smiles, and just like that, the show was over. Then it was time to head back and get ready for the night.

Brittany and her friend showed up at our room with what looked like the world's largest pizza. One slice got me full, despite it having been hours since I'd had a bite to eat. Brittany is the go-to woman for any and every night life event. She knows how to sharpen up a dull party. It didn't matter what the culture was. She really knows how to be herself and gives off that energy that you can't help but embrace. Now that the sun was tucked away and the moon glowing, it was time to have the experience of a lifetime.

City Walk was the name of the event we had purchased separately. It granted us access to all the clubs at no extra charge. The price of the ticket was a damn good deal.

"C'mon, c'mon, we're gon' do this club first, then this one, then this one," Brittany said.

I was down for whatever. There was a salsa club, a reggae club, a rap club, there were clubs for whatever you're into. We thought it was going to be large crowds, with everyone having fun. In each club we went to, the dance floor was either empty, or people got on it just to walk to the other side of the room. After we checked out all the clubs, we ended up staying at the reggae club the longest, since it was the most interesting one.

There was no one on the dance floor, but they had a live band playing reggaeton music. You couldn't help but feel the energy as they were playing. Brittany grabbed my hand to dance, but I kindly rejected, so she was on the floor dancing alone. Then I thought, *I did pay for this so I better enjoy while I can.* I got a couple shots and got out on the floor. My hips started to sway left and right, and I just let my body flow with the atmosphere of the music. Soon after everybody joined in. Reggaeton music creates a different type of vibe. How I would normally dance to rap music didn't fit the same type of vibe that they put off.

The next day was *Universal Studios*! Brittany and her friend decided to do something else. They didn't come with us. The park had more simulation rides than the other, but there was one roller coaster ride that knocked our socks off, *The Rip Rocket*. You can pick your own personal song through a choice of music each person had in their seat. The speakers were in the headrests, so you could be jamming away while your head sunk back due to the high speeds. You start off by going straight up and then, as you reach the highest peak, it becomes a non-stop adrenaline rush. It was the fastest ride they had out of both parks. It was short, but it's a ride that is worth waiting for.

After Samantha and I got off and were walking around, a guy caught our attention and told us how we could get money just by giving feedback. To me, that sounded too good to be true. Somebody is willing to pay people money for their feedback?

"No thank you."

We began to walk away.

"Hey, I know you think that I'm lying, but it's the truth."

"How will we receive the money? Cash or check?"

"You need to stick with this guy," he said, talking to Samantha, "he's a smart man. Y'all would get cash."

It was only $20, but for 15-20 minutes of our time answering questions on a computer it was a deal. To the both of us, it was worth it. I didn't see it at first, but they did have a sign up saying they would pay people money for their feedback. That alone should have attracted a lot of people. Many folks, like us probably thought the same thing… if it sounds too good to be true, it probably is. That's why they had a guy outside to convince people that it was actually true. It was open to any and everyone 18 or older. You go inside a building and sit down at one of their computers to give feedback.

After that, we went walking around to see what food they had to offer. Turkey legs! That was something I had never tried, even though the opportunity was presented to me many times. My taste buds are picky, like a kid's. I'm not about to eat something that came off a turkey, but I would eat something that came off a chicken. I needed to reprogram my train of thought. Staring at them great big ole legs made my mouth water. They looked perfectly cooked and seasoned. The price was not of my concern, I had to have one. On my first bite, I fell in love. I needed to sit down and enjoy it. Samantha didn't want one. I'm guessing it wasn't lady-like for her. There were no forks or napkins to eat properly. It didn't bother me. I was in full barbarian mode chomping down on that leg, bite after bite with grease all around my mouth and pieces of turkey hanging from my lips.

"This is good! You sure you don't want one?" I asked.

"No."

She enjoyed eating her ice cream dots peacefully. I tried to clear the bone, but it was too much. I was defeated. There was still meat left on the bone that my stomach didn't have any more room for. Our appetite was satisfied.

We walked around some more to let our food digest. There was a Betty Boop store nearby that she just had to go in and look around. She always loved her. Her intentions weren't to buy anything. We were on a strict budget. The only time I like Betty Boop, is when Halloween comes around and the females dress up as her. That has always been a sight to see! Fishnet leggings that went along with the hills and a mini skirt. The top was the main attraction, seeing big breasts partially exposed. That would come neck and neck with females dressing up like nurses.

As we walked through the store, checking out different merchandise, I saw a coffee mug with a Betty Boop picture on it and at the bottom it read, *Samantha*. She didn't notice it as she was on the other side looking around. I always love to surprise her with gifts. She is easily pleased, and that's what makes my job of being the best boyfriend a simple one. There was no chance that I could buy it without her noticing. The line was too long to make a quick transaction without being noticed, but I had to find a way to buy it secretly. She needed the right distraction.

There was a lot of noise going on outside. We went to go check it out. A Minion Parade! People were dressed up like Minions and they even had Dru in the car he always drove, the rocket. I waited until she was fully focused on the distraction, then it was time for me to execute. “Wait right here. I have to use the restroom bad.” She fell for it. I went around the corner to the other entrance where she couldn’t see me. After grabbing the mug, I was in line about ten minutes. I never told her what I was going to the restroom to do. For all she knew, I could’ve been shitting out the delicious turkey leg I ate earlier. After my purchase was made, I stuffed it in my backpack and made sure to carry it around extra carefully and not forget it was in there. I left the store and caught the last moments of the parade.

“I thought you forgot where I was. You were taking so long.”

“Yeah, I like to take my time when I’m on the toilet.”

That went right over her head. That night, I slid it underneath her pillow when she wasn’t looking. I wasn’t going to tell her I bought it, I wanted to see how she would respond when she found out. She sat on the bed, then she got up. I gave little hints. It was like the tables had turned and she was playing with my emotions by not lifting the pillows.

“I got a surprise for you.”

“Hahaha. No you don’t. What is it?”

“You will find out soon, trust me.”

Then I could tell her mind began to wonder. Her eyes looked up at the ceiling, wide with curiosity, then back at me.

“I was with you the whole time. You are telling a lie.”

“No, I’m not. You will just have to wait and see.”

When it was time for bed she would notice it, because she always adjusts her pillows before she lays down. She got up off the bed to take a shower. After she was done, she sat on the bed without touching any of the pillows. My plan began to backfire. Any other time she would have found it by now. I was getting impatient. Thoughts began to run through my head, *What if she fell asleep never knowing she was sleeping on her gift? Should I put it somewhere else?* I gave up.

"Your surprise is somewhere on the bed."

She smiled as she started to lift the covers.

"Keep looking."

Then she lifted the pillows.

"Ta-daaaaa, about time. You been getting up and down without noticing it."

"*Awwwww…* when did you buy it?"

I told her how I managed to pull off the trick. She was amazed, and let's just say that the rest of the night was a night to remember.

Our last day arrived quicker than we all expected. There was a 100% chance of rain. The skies were cloudy, with no chance of the sun breaking through. We had already experienced *Island of Adventure* amusement park the first day we came, which meant it was time to see the shows we'd missed and hit our favorite rides again, like Harry Potter, Incredible Hulk, and Spiderman. It was nice to finally take our time and not rush trying to make the most out of our day.

I tried different food stands than I had before, and the rest of the time we just chilled. *C-c-c-crack Boommmm!* The sound of thunder let us know our time there would soon be over. I didn't want to leave because of thunder. I wanted to wait until it started pouring, but what I wouldn't do was get on a ride and have the chance of being stuck upside down because of technical difficulties due to the weather. The winds picked up, followed by a light rain drizzle. Minutes later, it stopped. Then all hell broke loose. *C-c-c-c-crack boommmm!* The rain felt like we were standing in the shower, right underneath the spout catching every drop. We tried to run and get shelter, but everywhere we looked the spots were packed. We managed to squeeze under the hotdog stand umbrella. The rain didn't seem like it wasn't going to let up. *C-c-crack boommmm!* There was a big flash of lightning. A voice came over the loudspeaker.

"Warning, warning, the park is now closed due to inclement weather. Warning, warning, the park is now closed due to inclement weather."

There was no other choice but to get drenched by the rain as we sprinted to the bus stop to wait for our shuttle. We were going to still meet up with the crew later that night to go out to the bars one last time.

We had finished off the night at the Hard Rock Café. It was karaoke night. I wanted to have an exciting experience doing karaoke, but my alcohol buzz had gone down. As the question went around the table of who was going to get on stage and sing, everyone gave negative responses. I gave it some thought and looked over the list of songs in a big black binder that they had to sing along with. A few of them I knew some of the words to, but not the entire song. There was one that caught my eye that I knew all too well - Rockstar, by Nickelback.

I rehearsed that song over and over in my head, then I made my mark on the clipboard to be called up to give my rockstar performance. The list was long. I had waited until the last minute and now the restaurant was closing. Since this was our last day, for me, it was about experiencing things I'd never done and always wanted to do… like going to the Hard Rock Café and singing karaoke. But I ran out of time. Overall, our trip was a success, despite getting rained out of the park.

Now everyone was back in their hotel rooms. Samantha and I shared moments of our trip before crashing into a coma-like sleep. The next morning, we didn't go down for breakfast. We wanted to sleep in but couldn't. We still had to leave before our check out time to catch our flight. After fighting to get up to catch our shuttle, we managed to make it on time.

At the airport, we got through security quickly by using all the tricks they taught me - wear flip-flops and already have your possessions in hand. I took one last walk around, looking at everything. Soon after that, we were boarding the plane. The plane ride was quick. Before we knew it, there was a message over the intercom,

"This is your captain speaking. You have now arrived at Nashville, TN International Airport BNA."

Their sister came to pick us up and we headed home. Nothing else to do but to unpack and snap back into reality. I quit my job as a janitor. My school schedule wouldn't allow me to do both. I left on a good note, planning to *never* return. Not that being a janitor is bad, but it isn't aligned with my destiny. It was just a job to get me over some hurdles. The only things that were occupying my schedule from then on out were going to work at Duewell Electric and apprenticeship school.

CHAPTER 17
WHAT DO ELEPHANTS EAT? DEEZ NUTS

Granny's health started to get bad, so bad that she could barely talk. I thought I could take my time getting to know her and enjoy what it was like having a granny. That taught me a lesson. When the opportunity comes for you to meet someone, and you feel like you can have a strong connection with that person, don't sit on the fence. Get to know them for who they really are. You never know if you will see them again.

Some of my friends have grannies, and my son does on his mother's side. I see how my son and his granny act around each other and it's nothing out of the ordinary, but it's always been something I wanted to feel for myself. I grew up without a dad, but not once did I worry about his whereabouts. My mother was my father also, but she couldn't be my granny. She'd taught me how to be respectful, independent, and never back down from anyone.

I wanted to see granny's fun side and hear her stories about back in the day to get a history lesson. What clubs were poppin'? What bars were her favorite to go to? How many fights had she gotten into? I wanted her to spill all the juice. I realized I would never have answers to those questions coming from her point of view.

I passed my third-year class with excellence. May 5, 2015 is when I started my 4th year of apprenticeship school. I could have held out on going to summer school, and waited for the next semester to enroll, but I wanted to go ahead and get it out of the way. It wasn't going to interfere with my summer plans. My hunger for summer vacation had already been fulfilled by going to Florida. Rumor on the job was that if anybody ever got Mr. Evans for their fourth year, he was going to make sure they passed. Every student that had him said he was the most informative and so much cooler than all the other teachers.

When I got my fourth-year schedule and saw his name as my teacher, I knew the summer would be better spent going to school than waiting. Not everybody transitioned over to summer classes, though. If you didn't pass his class, it's because you didn't want to. He made things so easy, even the things that we thought were complicated when first looking at them. He was a teacher that made sure everyone understood what he was teaching. To me, it seemed like teaching electrical was his top priority with how seriously he took it. Those that chose not to go to summer school would miss the experience of being with him. His classes were only in the summer, so the decision was a no-brainer.

By far, he was the best apprenticeship teacher at that school. I passed my fourth and final year of being an electrical apprentice. I was a certified Journeyman Electrician! I just had to wait for the official graduation to receive my card and certificate to have proof of my accomplishment. Summer school flew by quick. I was so glad that I had my priorities straight, because the people that didn't go had to enroll in the next semester.

Back at work, a guy I knew that once worked for the same company called me and wanted me to work with him. I was planted firmly where I was though, and wasn't trying to leave my current job. Since I was then an electrician, I was certain they were going to bump my pay up to the electrician entry level - a $5 increase.

"Let me find out first if this company will give me the proper raise that I deserve," I said.

"I'm telling you, they are not going to give you that amount of money in one raise."

"I hear what you saying, but I still want to find out for myself."

That's the Taurus in me - bull-headed, never taking anyone else's word but my own. What's the worst that could possibly happen? They tell me no? Sure, if so, then I had another opportunity with a different company that was waiting on me.

"Okay, but if they don't, give me a call back. I'm guaranteeing you I can get you hired on making more money here. That's why I left that Duewell Electric."

"Okay, I will give you a call later to let you know my answer."

I was earning $13 per hour at the time, as a Top Helper. I never received a raise while going to school. A $5 jump was unheard of, but $18 was the starting pay of an entry level electrician. I knew this day would come, and that's why I tried to be a sponge and soak up all the knowledge that spilled out in front of me. I didn't want them to come up with an excuse for not paying me what I deserved. Everyone who worked with me knew how hard of a worker I was.

When it was time to talk with my boss about a raise, I was aware the entry level pay was too far out of my reach with this company. I asked my foreman if he could talk to the superintendent to bump my pay up to $17, not $18 per hour. Even though I should ask for $18, a dollar less wouldn't seem that bad. He started to ask me questions,

"What do these symbols mean on the blueprint? What blueprint is needed to check for ceiling height, etc?"

I answered all of them correctly.

"Well, you know… $17 per hour is kinda-sorta in the ballpark of what you should be making."

I thought, what the hell does kinda-sorta mean? He knew that was on the low end of being an entry level electrician.

"I been with this company for two years, and not once received a raise. Even with me finishing school."

"You know, we don't have to give a raise just because you graduated."

"Naw, I didn't know. I figured they would since I'm proven to the company, I'm taking this career field seriously."

"I will spread the word, but I'm not guaranteeing that you will get that much."

"Okay."

Right then, I knew my pay rate was *not* going to increase. My coworker got a raise after completing his third year… and it was only ten cents. Not fifty cents, not a dollar, only ten cents. I called my previous coworker back when I had time and told him I was all-in. He pulled some strings. The boss of that company, Cornwell Electric, called me up the next day after work. I told him about my experience, and why I was looking to switch companies due to company lack advancement opportunities. He understood. When asked how much I was looking to make, I told him $20 per hour. I knew it was a lot, but I didn't want to get underpaid ever again. Making that much would mean I know I was getting the top pay—and then some—for my level of experience, but I also knew that I wouldn't be getting another raise for a long time, which was fine by me. I wasn't looking to retire at an electrical company anyways, not unless it was my own. He scheduled an interview with me to talk more about the pay rate.

The day of the interview, we made a deal. He was going to start me out at $16 per hour, then after thirty days of me proving what I knew, it would increase to $18. Just like that, I was in. He understood me wanting to give my two-week notice so no bridges would be burnt. I felt some type of way about the deal at first. *What if, after the thirty days, he went back on his word*? On the bright side, it was still $3 more than what I was making with Duewell Electric.

After being with that company and proving to them, and myself, that I was just as a hard worker as anyone else, it was time to quit. I needed something other than a pat on the back for completing school. The more knowledge you have, the more money you should receive. There weren't too many people that took the advantage of staying late or coming in on weekends to get some overtime like I did. And I always asked questions, showing my eagerness to learn. Plus, while going to school, I *never ever* complained when I finished my third year and didn't see an increase on my paycheck. *Oh well*, I thought, *it will be on there at the end of my fourth year*. Wrong again. I came into work and gave my boss the two-week notice before even asking if he'd tried to talk to the superintendent. He didn't care. The work continued like normal, and I was relieved. I'd gotten what I needed out of that company, which was the education and experience, and it was time to go off to my next adventure in life.

At Cornwell Electric, I was working the night shift. This company had most of the Kroger contracts for remodeling around surrounding cities of Nashville. It was easy and laid back. The adjustment from working during the day to night was hard. At the beginning, I would come home and go straight to bed, only to wake up due to my alarm clock letting me know it was time to do it all over again. All through the day, I was sleeping like a baby. That went on for two weeks. The only time that I would fight my sleep to stay up was when I had important errands to run.

Just like at my old job when there was an opportunity to get overtime, I always volunteered… even though I didn't want to. I didn't need the extra money like I did when I was working for Duewell Electric. It was the attitude to come in with a team player work ethic that could earn me more money on the hour. Even with overtime, the days seemed to go by quick. My mind was focused on the end of my thirty-day probationary period. When I reached my big day, the boss kept his word and granted me $2 extra. I had reached my goal.

But it didn't last. Not even a year passed before I was fired from Cornwell Electric. Why? They couldn't give me a good enough reason. After that, my life began to spiral downhill. My car was a money pit. Every time I took it to the shop to get it fixed, something else would happen. My relationship took a wrong turn as well.

One morning, Samantha gave me money to pay the light bill. My wallet couldn't cover the cost. I was heading out anyway, and told her that I would take care of it. I was fed up with going through different emotions from the highs and lows that life brought me. I thought of a plan to blow all my past worries up in smoke. I'm talking about a big cloud. She was struggling for that month. I knew that but I was too blinded by misery to care. My struggles brought my mentality into a selfish mode.

I called up Charlie, an old friend, to pick me up. He is the guy that would always come around if you got something to smoke, but when you don't, he can never be found. That's why I would rarely chill with him. I just needed somebody to vent to while I smoked.

Samantha wasn't against smoking; she just didn't do it herself. He came to pick me up, and we left. First stop, go to see the weed man. I bought a big bag to satisfy all my struggles and worries. Long-term. His eyes grew wide when he saw the amount I bought.

"*Damnnn!* We about to smoke all of that?"

"I'm gonna try to."

"You my dawg."

"Yeah, I'm only your dawg when there's weed involved."

"What?"

"You heard me."

We went to the riverside of my favorite park, where little to no people ever went. If there were some people down there, they would be fishing. They would be focused on catching fish and not us. We were smoking blunts back-to-back in the comfort of his vehicle. The sky was clear, and the sun was shining. Not too hot or too cold, my day was perfect. There was no chance of smoking the whole bag. We had been there for hours, and it still was half full.

"I just thought of a joke," I said, "why did the elephant go into the boy's restroom?"

He thought for a second.

"Aw, because he wanted to get high. Ahh hahahaha! That was a good one."

"Hahahaha! Naw fool. It went into the boy's restroom to get some nuts. Get it? Elephants like nuts."

"Bahahaha! You too silly. Wait a minute, I don't get it. You said elephants like nuts, then why it picked the boy's restroom?"

"Because boys have nuts, duhhhh!"

"Yeah, but they the little ones. Why didn't it go into the men's room, so it can get some big nuts, not the little baby ones? The elephant will never get full eating baby nuts."

"Bahahaha! Congratulations, my fellow US Citizen. Our brains are now fried. Hahahahaha! Yup, it's time to go. Stop by the liquor store so I can pick me up a quarter pint."

It was a quick in and out. I didn't let him drink any right there because he was driving. I trusted him smoking and driving though because he always took the backroads so he could cruise.

"Bet you I can chug all of this before we get to the house."

It took me over five times to get down the whole bottle, but I felt complete when it was finished. I was trash from that point forward. We made it back to the house in one piece.

"Let me hold some of that."

"*What?!* I just smoked all of Mary Jane… plus some of her cousins with you, and you still asking for more? Naw, you good. See ya later."

I hid the rest of it in the backseat of my car before I walked in the house. Samantha was in the kitchen, cooking.

"Hey babe, I'm cooking your favorite."

"Okay, I'm about to lay down."

"You okay? What's wrong?

"I'm fine," I said, while walking away.

I flopped down face first on the bed. She could sense something was wrong. Usually, we greet each other with either a kiss, hug, slap on the ass, or something else that has to do with touching each other. This time was different. It was in the middle of the day, and there I was trying to sleep. She came in the room.

"*Ewwww!* You smell like a skunk."

"We must have passed by one when he was driving *hahahaha*."

"Are you high?"

"I think so. I feel good."

At this point, I knew she figured everything out. It was time for me to come clean. There was no hiding the smell, or my level of highness.

"Terrance McAdoo, please tell me you didn't do what I think you did."

Whenever she said my first and last name in the same sentence, she meant business. I paused for quite some time. My thoughts were backed up in the corner. There was no way to make it sound sweet without being dishonest. I turned over to face her.

"Baby… I'm sorry. I really am. You know all the stress I been through lately. I was wanting to find an escape."

Both of her fists were clenched tight. Her eyes were locked in with mine, and her nose drew up causing it to wrinkle. It was the right time for my body to be numb, because I was about to get the shit beat out of me. I laid there, feeling paralyzed.

"That was the money to get caught up on the light bill. It was already late," she began to walk towards me, "and you blew it just to get high? Don't you know they are going to cut my lights off tomorrow if I don't pay them today? That was all the money I had." She was now standing over me.

"Mom, the food is burning!" one of the kids yelled.

"Stay right here. I'm not done with you."

As soon as she walked out, I forced myself out of bed to use the bathroom. I had been holding it for a while and didn't want to get out of my comfort spot. She came back in as I was heading back to the bed. Her next two words left me devastated. I couldn't believe that after all we had built together, we would be separated. No time for jokes. This was real. I loved her, but I had been willing to put our relationship on the line for temporary pleasure. Not long-term thinking. It wasn't worth it. I was reaping the consequences of my actions. The two words that she told me weren't the two words you're thinking. They were the two words that would put me back in the abyss, leaving me nowhere to go or turn to. The two words were not "it's over," they were,

"Get out!" she yelled.

"What?! No. Where am I supposed to go? You know my car is about to break down."

"Not my problem. You should have thought about that while you were smoking. You can leave your stuff here for a little while, until you find a proper spot. And I will even pack it up for you. But you… you… you such a dumbass. After all that I did for you…" she paused, as tears began to well up in her eyes, and her voice started to crack, "I would have laid down my life for you, but not anymore."

"C'mon ba—"

She quickly interrupted me.

"No. I don't think you can call me baby anymore. Terrance McAdoo, you need to leave."

I stood there thinking of what to say.

"Nowwwwwwwww!!!"

She raised her right hand and pointed me to the exit.

"I'm out."

She walked me to the front door. Right when I stepped outside, *wham!* she kicked me in the nuts. I tried to stay a man and play it off like it didn't hurt. I just had to hunch over a little bit while holding my nuts as I walked. I made it to my car, where I sat for a moment trying to get my pain under control. My car smelt like a skunk community. Since there was nothing else to do, I thought it would be a good time to get higher. I'm talking about an out-of-body experience. It started to rain. Hard.

Whenever I'm in my car chilling, either listening to music or getting stoned, if it starts raining during one of those moments, it takes my level of meditation to another universe. If it was thunder and lightning, it would be the opposite. In this situation, it was just a downpour of rain. Somehow, I knew I would be okay.

After renewing my membership to the "Mountain High Club." I was so high that I fell asleep sitting in my car. When I woke back up, I called Brittany to see if I could stay with her. I didn't tell her everything, just the important stuff like, "me and your sis just got into a heated argument, and I need somewhere to calm down." She agreed I could come over. I drove across the street to her house. I had nothing to shield myself from the rain. I got out of the car and ran up her porch steps. I made it to the last step when my foot got caught. Instantly, a certain someone paid me a visit. Her name was "Karma" and her shirt read, *I'm a bitch.* I stumbled, trying to catch my balance... *bam!* I face planted the front door and fell. Brittany opened the door,

"Get up! I oughta kick you in the head."

After entering the house, she stopped me in my tracks,

"Samantha already told me what happened before you called. I know you a good person and really didn't mean no harm. The only reason why I'm doing this is for one, you have no where else to go, and two, you are family."

When she said that, it let me know I had been forgiven. My face still hurt like a *muthafucka,* even still being on Cloud 9. She already knew about me smoking and didn't care as long as it wasn't in the house.

The next day, the electric company came by to do their job. Samantha's lights got cut off. Words couldn't explain how I felt seeing that, and knowing that her kids had to suffer as well because of me. That was my ultimate punishment, having to sit and watch my stupidity all unfold in front of my eyes. Luckily, she had a friend lend her money to have her lights cut back on by the end of the night.

Brittany had an extra bedroom that I could use, so I stayed in the back part of her house. It was already set up with a bed, lamp, dresser, TV, everything I needed to feel comfortable. She didn't have any kids, it was just an extra room for when guests wanted to sleep over. There was another room that could be used as a bedroom, but it was used for storage space. Now that I had a new place to stay at, it was a matter of when it would be safe to get my stuff. When Samantha went to work was when I went in and got my things. She wasn't playing, all my stuff was packed and waiting for me by the door. Maybe she would forgive me, maybe not. I had to focus on getting myself a job. A whole month had passed since we last talked, and during that time that raggedy car of mine decided to take its last breath. Just when I thought I was *Found in My World,* I became uncertain again.

Life was steadily dealing me blow after blow, yet I kept rising, but this one was going to take me a while to get back up from. How would I get back on my feet without a car to get me a job so I could start living again? I love the feeling of being independent and hate the feeling of asking someone to help me. I don't like to feel like I'm a burden. How could I be a grown man when I had to have a roommate to survive? On top of that, I didn't even have any money to help with the bills. Brittany became the mother, and I was the child getting taken care of.

Week after week went by without having a conversation with Samantha. Thoughts started to arise,

Maybe she's waiting on me to make the first move. What if she's talking to someone else already? Will she ever take me back? Would it be a good move if I texted her to see how she's doing? What if I text her to see, and she don't respond?

Brittany wouldn't give me the info on Samantha's love life. She already told me that's between me and Samantha, and that she was not going to get involved in any kind of way. Everything was put on me to try to make it right. Somedays, I sat on the porch for hours to see if another man would pull down her driveway. That never happened. All the good and lustful memories we had together kept playing over and over in my head. It was a struggle falling asleep not having someone to hold. The only way to ease the pain of my thought process was to get the closure that I needed. Curiosity got the best of me, and eventually led me to go over to her house and ask her where we would go from there.

When I made it to her house and knocked on the door, her kid answered and told me to come in. I proceed with caution, thinking that it might be a set-up. That would be bad to walk in and get struck by a throwing star or stabbed with a ninja sword, but there she sat, on the bed in her room watching old reruns of her favorite show, *Girlfriends.* She turned around when her son told her it was me. When her eyes looked up at me, I stopped dead in my tracks. Then she turned back around to finish watching her show.

"Can I have a hug… please?" I asked.

She stood up and gave me one, then sat back down. It was one of the most awkward moments I'd ever felt. She didn't crowd me with questions or concerns about why it had taken so long for me to see her. When I tried to speak, she paused me,

"Shhh, not right now."

There was no need to rush a conversation. The big prize was me sitting next to her. We chatted for a bit during the commercial breaks, but when the show came back on it was quiet time. There were only brief windows of communication during the commercial breaks, so my questions had to be clear and concise.

"I thought you broke up with me."

"When did I say that? I don't *think* you can call me baby anymore is what I said, and I kicked your ass out 'cause I was having scary thoughts about what I wanted to do to you. But I will always love you, come here."

She grabbed my shirt and pulled me towards her. "Mwah… don't do that to me *ever* again."

Her eyes were locked on mine, and it seemed like she was staring into my soul.

"Yes ma'am."

We began to talk about random things, then I was interrupted.

"*Shh*, my show is back on."

Our relationship was rekindled, and we became love birds again.

We men sometimes get the feeling our girl is cheating when we do wrong, because of our guilty conscience. Sometimes that's not the case at all. Most couples do get revenge, that's the day and age we are living in right now. There is a tiny percentage of women that don't look at themselves that way because it's not ladylike to sleep around with different men, especially to get revenge. But she wasn't even thinking about me, or any other person. I think she knew my ass wasn't going anywhere because of what she provided me during our relationship. She would occasionally cook me breakfast in bed, complete with fresh cut fruits. Whether it was money, sex, or being a sounding board to vent my problems to, she was always there. Simple things like walks in the park were enough to keep her satisfied. She is authentic. My chances of finding another woman like her would seem very slim to me. The whole time I was worrying about her leaving me, she was only getting in tune with her show, *Girlfriends*. Even though we were back cool, I wasn't trying to stay in her house anymore. Her sister's was peaceful with only her living there, and most of the time she was gone dancing. She understood. Samantha and I would always joke about getting married, and I decided that I was going to put it in action soon. I didn't know if she would give me the yay or nay, but it would be worth a shot. She isn't materialistic at all; it's the simple things that she cares about. "It's not about the price tag but the thought that counts," is what she'd say.

Ladonna was moving hours away from where she once lived, and asked if I could keep my son. I wasn't in a situation to take care of him, I could barely take care of myself, but he was my responsibility and not anyone else's. I agreed. We went to court, filled out all the paperwork, and were sworn in by the judge. Everything went smoothly. The judge granted me temporary custody until she got me back in court to file joint custody. I was hoping that time would never come. She is a great mother, but I wanted him to grasp onto something positive like sports and not end up running the streets and going nowhere in life. I knew how to work him to become an independent man, and not stay a dependent child. Even though I'd made careless decisions in the past, I knew how he could avoid similar problems. Women love to baby their boys, but he needed to learn the ins and outs of life from my mistakes and a man to raise him. I didn't feel like a man at the time, but I knew I would one day bounce back. If you fall, you must pick yourself back up because life will walk all over you and not think twice, but only if you lay down and allow it to keep you there.

Brittany cleared out the room she was using for storage space, so he was good in there. My circumstances were hard the way they were, and they seemed to be getting even harder with me having to raise him full time now. I called up Samantha. She usually had encouraging words to help settle my mind whenever it was filled with uncertainty.

He understood the situation and was okay with it. There were friends that he already had in my neighborhood by visiting on the weekends. It didn't take long for him to get settled in. I got him enrolled in his new school, and everything went according to plan on his part. Mine was still under construction.

CHAPTER 18
DOWNGRADE

June 2, 2016 was the official day for the graduation ceremony from the apprenticeship school. Samantha let me borrow her car, and I brought my son with me. At least at this graduation I wouldn't be alone. She didn't come because of her kids. The traditional graduation music wasn't played. It wasn't even held at a special location. All the graduates sat in this big room at the school, with tables all around to accommodate the guests. There weren't many graduates. We ate our food, got our certificates of completion, certified electrician cards, took pictures, and that was the end. Mr. Brent told me that Joe, the school director, had been fired. That was good news to my ears. He did a horrible job, and glad that's over with.

It was now time to focus on getting my life back on track by saving up to get a car, someway, somehow. I had been applying for electrical jobs that would give me a company vehicle. My application was rejected by all of them. I was a rock stuck in a hard place. With time on my hands to do whatever, I proceeded to write my first book. At least that would balance out my stress level of being in the house all day. I decided to go to the unemployment office to get government assistance, and a job. My application was accepted for food stamps and a weekly paycheck, but only if I showed proof that I had been out looking for a job on a weekly basis. Online was my only chance of getting work.

There was an opening for lawn care services. That was a huge downgrade from my professional career. I didn't like it at all. From learning about electrical theory, to maintaining the grass seemed like taking one-hundred steps backwards. This was all they had though, and to get back on my feet I had to play the *cards that were dealt.* The owner of the lawn care company always went to the unemployment office to pick up applications. He just so happened to give me a call for an interview. The interview went well, and I got hired. It wasn't a guaranteed forty-hour paycheck every week, but it would still mean money. The upside of not getting a forty-hour paycheck was that I could still get my unemployment checks, because it didn't exceed the limit. I knew there wouldn't be a problem with getting to work, because I could get dropped off where everyone met in the mornings at the gas station. Brittany and Samantha's business slowed down tremendously. That freed up some of her time, so she could drop me off and pick me back up.

On my first day, I was handed a weed eater. I was thinking it would be easy just to hold it and walk. Little did I know, there was a real learning curve to doing it. If you don't hold it the right way, the trimming would get messed up causing patches in the grass. I was thinking about it being a downgrade from my career field at first, but then I thought, *this is what's helping me sew my life back together.* The first school we cut wasn't that bad, but the second one was challenging because I wasn't told about breaks. The normal work schedule on most jobs is a 15-minute break at 9 a.m. and lunch at 12 p.m. When I looked at my watch and saw that it had passed 9 a.m., my body was ready for a break. The sun began to heat up, causing my energy to evaporate. They were still working, and there I was struggling to keep up the pace. When we all met back up in a group, a crew of five people including me, I asked them when the break times were,

"You take a break whenever you get tired," the lead guy said.

It was only me and another guy on the weed eaters, and everyone else had a riding lawn mower. By 12 p.m., my body was drenched with sweat. It felt like football conditioning all over again at the peak of summer! But I'm no quitter. I was going to tough it out till the end. The school that we'd previously mowed had nothing on Maplewood High School. It was a marathon cutting their grass. Not only did we have to cut everything around their school, but also both football fields.

I tried to take as many breaks as I could without leaving my partner doing all the work, but he was consistent. We all wanted to get done so we could go home. It was our last job for the day. I kept chugging along, but at a slow pace. When the other crews finished their schedule, they came to help. It would take all night to cut their fields and around the school with just one crew. Depending on where we were at in the cutting, determined how many crews it would take to finish at a reasonable time. Usually, it would be one other crew that helped.

At the end, I was totally exhausted and ready to go home and take a nap. My hand was still shaking from the vibration of holding the weed eater all day. That was common, as my crew members told me that they experienced the same thing on their first day. I needed to gain weight, not lose it. I was already thin. If this job helped me to survive then so be it, I would do whatever it took.

The next day, I didn't have a ride to make it in the morning. Samantha unexpectedly had to be somewhere else and had told me the day before. I woke up to my alarm. My body felt like it had been in an Evander Holyfield fight. It was sore all over. The boss's number was in my phone, but I didn't inform him that I wasn't going to make it to work that day. It would sound bad if I had called him and asked if somehow, someone would be willing to pick me up to work. My body needed time to recuperate anyway, so I didn't bother. My bed was my sanctuary, and I went back to sleep. Then my phone started to ring. It was the main boss, the owner of the company! He wanted to know if I had quit. I surely wanted to tell him yeah, but figured he would handle that for me when he found out I didn't have dependable transportation. The crew probably gave him good news about how I did my first day because he insisted on picking me up himself and dropping me off at work. I texted him my address and he showed up.

That was strange. *If he knew I didn't have dependable transportation, then why would he still want me on the job?* I knew he wouldn't be able to pick me up every morning, and Samantha sometimes had personal errands she had to take care of. I couldn't depend on her to drop me off every morning like I had initially thought. The following day was when she would be available. He never asked if this would be a frequent problem or not. It might be the first and only time he picked me up, I didn't know. I wasn't confident that I would be able to make it on time every day, or even show up at all. My thought was to roll with what I got and cross that bridge when I get to it.

My partner informed me the worst was yet to come. Our last stop of the day was McGavock High School. It was the biggest school on everybody's job list to cut, as one of the top three largest public schools in Nashville. We usually started in the late morning, around 10 a.m. This time I was prepared for the heat. I got me a big jug and filled it up with ice and water before I left the house. On the job, it seemed like it was never going to end. Same as Maplewood, we worked around the school and ball fields. Even with two crews working at that location, it still seemed like it took forever to finish.

I couldn't wait to get my ass on a riding mower. It wasn't always gravy on their side, but it was better than holding a weed eater and walking for miles, never knowing when the road would end. It just keeps going and going and going. Even though we weren't the only two weed eating, it still was a struggle to maintain a steady pace. We climbed hills, moved benches, and navigated other obstacles to get a nice clean cut. It had to be the last cut of the day. I thought it was always going to be the same schedule. Get the small jobs done quickly, then all the crews meet up to tackle the biggest job. We took our afternoon lunch for thirty minutes, then got back to it. It was challenging coming back from lunch then continuing where you left off on a job that big. Unfortunately, it wasn't the last job of the day. There were still other jobs we had to do. Not nearly as big, though.

The biggest job the lawn company had—and the one that made countless people quit on the same day—was a beast. It would be a challenge for me. It would stretch my abilities to another level. For some, they had to experience it on their first day. The two high schools had nothing on this, even if they were combined. Even the owner contributed. He always had his boots on the ground, doing light work like mulch and planting, but we needed everybody on deck when it came to this location. It would prove if you had what it takes to be a lawn care employee at this company. My crew warned me ahead of time, but I thought they were over exaggerating and just trying to scare me.

When they gave me the run-down about *Nashville International Airport*, I thought surely we weren't doing the whole thing… so, what's the big deal? My mindset was around the airport where the terminals are. Now that I knew I could take a break whenever, it didn't seem all that hard. Better believe I took frequent breaks in the shade! I wasn't about to be a macho man by trying to hold off on my breaks thinking, we can finish quicker by taking less breaks. This was a full team effort. It took a full day to complete, depending on which part of the airport we were doing. Some locations took two days. By having already experienced the worst, I knew what to expect and could manage my workload without overdoing it.

The following weeks became a breeze to me, and not a headache. They had a high turnover rate due to the airport job alone. The people in my crew would do a friendly bet on who would last the longest every time we got someone new. The airport was what determined how hard of a worker any new guy was going to be. If you could come back after spending time on that job, then the other jobs would be simple. One of my co-workers lived right down the street from me and we had never crossed paths before. We figured that out when he asked me where I lived. I gave him the street name. He agreed to pick me up in the mornings and take me back home, since my ride wasn't 100% dependable. That helped a bunch, so that was my ride.

My plan was to save as much money as possible and combine it with my income tax return to buy my next car with cash. With the help of government assistance, I was doing a whole lot of saving. I would spend less than half of my work check, because my food stamps covered the food. I helped out with what I could by paying the cheapest bills at Brittany's place. All the pieces to my life puzzle started to fit back together.

I survived through the punishing, sizzling summer heat. October was the last month of cutting grass. When we reached the end, there was nothing else for us to do due to the grass starting to die out. We all got laid off.

Thanksgiving had arrived, and I was invited to Samantha's family gathering. Everyone knew about me, they just hadn't met me yet. My son spent the holiday with his mom. I was skeptical of going at first, since I'd be the only Black person there, but then I was quickly reminded of all the food that was going to be there. We hardly kept anything in the fridge. It was a situation that I needed to deal with, since I would be around for a while. I needed to get used to them as well, and they'd need to get used to me coming around on special holidays. When we arrived, it felt no different from being with my actual family. They treated me as if they had known me for years. There was no side eye, staring, or uncommon questions. Everybody acted how they normally would, despite all the drama with racial issues that were currently going on around. Both of our levels of hospitality were the same. Equal balance. Nobody is better than anyone, and that's how they treated me.

After praying over the food, it was time to grub. The food was amazing, with plenty of cookies, cakes, brownies… you name it, and it was there. Then the host of the gathering said something that brought me back to my roots.

"Hey, y'all take as many to-go plates as you can."

That was all I needed to hear. It felt comfortable taking as many to-go plates that could fit in both of my grocery sacks. When mom cooked, whenever there's leftovers, she wanted it all gone. That means less food to put up, and that would leave room for what you really wanted to eat, like desserts. I came to realize that everyone was doing the same thing. The family didn't have as much as me, but most walked out of there with at least one plate in their hand. The holiday was a success.

December 31, 2016, was when I celebrated bringing in the new year at one of their friend's house. It was a small group of people. We did the usual - drinking, listening to music, and playing beer pong. I knew what beer pong was but had never played it. They went over the rules with me, and I became a "professional" overnight, with the help of my partner. That evening, we never lost a game. Beer Pong Champions! Everyone did the New Year's countdown, took another shot, then left. I rode back home with Samantha to end the night off with a *bang!*

I had her pistol in the car, the one that she had bought for her birthday. It was fully loaded, and I wanted to leave a mark on the year. It's almost like a tradition to shoot your gun on New Year's Day. We pulled up in her driveway. My mind was racing back and forth of letting off the whole clip. We could hear different gunshots in the neighborhood. That boosted me up even more to let it rip. I knew she wouldn't like it, but January 1st comes once a year. I would just blame it on the liquor. I reached under the seat to grab it without telling her what was about to go down. If she would have noticed what was about to happen, she would've talked me out of it. As soon as I got out the passenger side door, I cocked it back and let the bullets fly. *Pow! Pow! Pow!* All thirteen shots.

"Terrance McAdoo! Are you serious!?"

I looked at her, with a big grin, "What? I know you hear everyone else shooting."

She closed the car door and headed inside. She didn't tell me that I couldn't come in, so I went in the house behind her and still had a great night cap. I'd had some good relationships in my past, but she topped them all, *easily*. She told me, after walking in the park on a gorgeous Sunday afternoon, that I was the best man she had ever loved. The only thing that was an issue was the kids. *Could I handle the workload of taking care of all of them, plus mine?* Only time would tell.

Fast forward a few months later, and my tax refund had been deposited in my bank. I took all my money to put towards a car. I had already done my research on what car to get. It couldn't be any car. I really had to plan this out. It needed to be a car that I could easily work on by myself and do regular maintenance to save money while also having a good car rating. I narrowed my search by going on the computer to see which car lot had an Impala from the years 2010 through 2012 that was in my price range. I traveled around to three car lots before I found the right one. YouTube was also helpful, because it helped me see what the key issues were with those cars that would normally come up, and how to fix them. It was an easy fix for the most common ones, but there were others that I had no choice but to let a mechanic fix.

After pulling up to the car lot and seeing the one that caught my eye, I did a vin number check. The dealer usually gives you this information, but I wanted to trust my own report. Some salesmen are untrustworthy these days. Everything looked good on the report. No accidents. I checked everything to make sure it was working right - brakes, any sign of oil leakage, weird noises that the engine might make, heating and air conditioning, even the CD player… everything! It was all the money I had, and this was a "sold as is" car lot, which meant no refunds or warranties. It was a nice car—had a sunroof and heated seats—but the only problem that stood out was the bad rotors. Their price was about the same as Kelley Blue Book. Since the rotors were bad, I talked him down a little bit more. He agreed to the price, and I handed the cashier the money and filled out the paperwork. It felt good to be back rolling again, but in style this time. I never had a car that was equipped with heated seats and a sunroof! What I settled for was a 2010 Chevy Impala, for $6000.

The time came back around to start working for the lawn care service again. I had already been filling out applications to get me back in my career field. It was only a matter of time before I got the call. That call never came before the start of the lawn care season, which is in March/April. I let my boss know that this would only be temporary until I could get hired by an electrical company, since I now had a car. The boss understood, and after a week or two went by I received a call. I was hired by a well-known electrical contractor that paid good on a weekly basis. My circumstances did a 180-degree turn, and I agreed to pay all of Brittany's bills every month since that would be the place my son and I would live.

A year after paying cold hard cash for my car, the transmission went out. They don't make cars like they used to. By having good money management skills, I had the money already sitting in the bank to get a rebuilt one that cost me $1,700. My pockets took a hit, but I still had a little bit left to get me through the week. It only took the mechanic three days to replace it. It was already a bad sign though, and I hoped it would be the last major problem.

Sometimes when me and Samantha went to the mall, we would stop at a couple jewelry stores. Not to get anything, just window shopping. On a beautiful day, we decided to get out and walk around the mall. We walked into a well-known store, just to have a peek.

"One day, I will be able to buy everything on this counter," I said, joking around.

I studied her style. She loved hearts. Instantly, the jeweler navigated her to the right section. She was in love with the one that stood out the most. It was a big diamond heart, with a smaller one in the center above it. The ring band was iced out with diamonds all around. That was it. Out of all the stores we went window shopping in, it was the ring that stood out the most. It went together well with both the engagement and the wedding ring. They both come together to form one gorgeous, unique ring. She loved it, and so did I.

The wedding ring that caught my eye was a silver one, with diamond cuts all around it, something unique and affordable. The jeweler wrote down the description of the two so that at any time either one of us could come and order the ring. She didn't know when or even if I was going to propose. It takes years of me being in a relationship with someone to make that big of commitment. But with this lady, I was thinking slightly about rushing the process. At any point in time, I could make the call and get it ordered.

We hadn't surprised each other in a long time. This surprise that I was about to pull would be like no other. There was never any major problem between us, just disagreements that we didn't let stick around. There want be any other perfect time than to do it on the same day that I came up with the idea. There were no plans for that day. It was Brittany, her, and I sitting around chilling in the mansion on a week her friend was going out of town and needed someone to dog sit.

"I'm about to head out right quick. I will be back," I said.

No questions were asked. No favors were suggested. I made it to Greenhill's Mall. I already knew she would love my gift that I was gonna present to her when I came back. The price tag was the right limit, not exceeding what was in my bank account. There was no hesitation about getting it. Her style was easy to choose from because she isn't picky at all. Even if her gift didn't come with a lot of sparkles to it, she would still be satisfied. No matter what, I didn't want to wait. I narrowed my search down to two items. From there, it was extremely hard to pick just one. It was pointless to buy two of the same things, even if it was a distinctive style. I took a wild guess and ended up picking one that she might like the most. It would be something that she would cherish for a lifetime. It didn't matter what our relationship status became in the future, she would think of me every time she wore it. I paid, grabbed the little baggy, and left.

I put the box in my pocket before walking in the house. There they stood, in the kitchen. Nobody knew what was about to happen. I got her attention, then walked up to her. I got down on one knee and reached in my pocket to get the box. She looked over at Brittany, Brittany looked back at her. Their eyes tried to process what was going on. I tried to get the box out but my pockets were too tight. I pulled and pulled till it came out. I wanted the presentation to flow smoothly, but oh well.

"Samantha Aaliyah Mitchell, will you be my…" I opened the box, "best friend forever?"

Both of them burst out laughing. She didn't even give me a yes or no.

"Thank you," she said, reaching for the box while laughing her heart out. It was glistening as the light reflected off it.

"Let me put it on you."

She handed it to me. It fit her perfectly.

I know it was a gift worth paying for. She stood there playing with it as the diamonds danced around her pendant. A silver necklace with a round diamond pendant and her birthstone in the center is what I got. Days later, it came back to me that I never did receive an answer when asking about her being my best friend forever. I reminded her of that. We both laughed.

"I'm sorry. Yes," she said, and gave me a kiss.

She was caught off guard, and I was more focused on her facial expression than the answer that night. Even though I wanted to get the ring, my conscience was telling me it was way too soon. We hadn't gone through any turbulence yet that would test our commitment. Long-term thinking. I always try to give her surprises, like trips that she would be unaware of. It was my way of testing out her spontaneous behavior. Most of the time, I knew her schedule and could plan a weekend trip in the blink of an eye. To see her brain trying to figure out where I was taking her was so exciting to me.

Question after question was asked. I would give little hints, but she still wouldn't catch on.

On one of my unexpected trips, we drove all the way to Ohio trying to locate a park in the city of Mason. There was no chance of making it in one day. Once we reached Cincinnati downtown, we parked to explore. It was a ghost town. There we were, in the middle of the night, with nobody around. Not even any cars. We were an interracial couple, walking the streets like we owned them. We started to think maybe this was a bad time of night to be outside. We were tourists, and you could tell. Both of us were amazed taking pictures at the different sculptures they had displayed throughout the area. When our "personal private tour" was over, we drove to find a spot to sleep for the night.

There was an abandoned truck stop right next to a gas station that we parked in for the night. I had gotten used to sleeping in a car. She had slept in a car before also, so this was nothing new to her. There were no other spots around that were close. I wanted to save money by not getting a room so we could cash out where I was taking her. Down the street from where we were, it looked like a dangerous neighborhood. Every other house was boarded up, and had their windows busted out. Our bloodline must have switched somehow that night. She wasn't worried at all. Minutes after we parked, she was out cold and snoring. But I was nervous thinking somebody was watching and planning to rob us. I grew up in rough neighborhoods. It's me that was supposed to be the one sleeping peacefully, not her. I got some rest in, but not much. When the morning came, we reached our destination at King's Island amusement park. As we pulled up to the entrance, she was excited. She never knew where I was taking her. Every ride that I got on, didn't matter how tall or fast it went, she was right beside me. Sometimes there was begging involved in order for her to get on, but the end result was a success. She was down for whatever. At the end of our extravaganza, we went to the welcome center in Ohio to sleep because I didn't have enough money for a motel room. She didn't mind. That's what I mean, she was down for whatever. Not many females would sleep in a car for a day on a random pop-up trip.

CHAPTER 19
BOTTOM LINE

The cards that have been dealt to me weren't easy to play, and I still have a lot more living and learning to do. I never thought that I would have experienced being homeless. It was my own fault for Kiesha kicking me out. For that, I felt that I was an outsider and wasn't going to talk to my immediate family ever again. My world got dark and lonely after that. Who wants to tell their friends that they're homeless? How will they respond? Will they keep it to themselves? We rarely got together, but when we did, it would be only for a brief period. They were always doing the same thing - either smoking, gambling, or just chilling on the block. It still wasn't enough to keep my mind off being homeless. I'm not the type of guy that always dresses in fancy clothes, but they were decent, so my selection of clothes didn't change.

Being homeless always played in the back of my mind, like when I could no longer keep up with my side of the rent that I owed to Kiesha which led me to being out on the streets. When I was put in the loneliest stage in my life, it was a matter of figuring out how I was going to survive. And doing it alone. There was no other means of support whatsoever. Those circumstances would be scary to most people, but for me, it was almost as if I had been preparing for a long time for it.

Tracy was the girl that I wanted. She wasn't in a relationship with anyone at the time, but was pregnant with her second child. That was something that I was willing to deal with. She was a good mother. She had all the bells and whistles that came along with that like, cooking, cleaning, being a caregiver, etc. With the combination of us two, I felt as if we could conquer anything. But Tracy wasn't the one. She had all the attributes any good man could want, but she found love in in the same spot where she had to defend and protect herself from her own kind.

I was looking to better her circumstances, not stay in the same spot where she had to defend and protect herself from her own kind.

If I wasn't going to stay under her roof then I was going to find my own living arrangements my old house, even though I had to break into it. The basement wasn't the ideal place for me to live, but it was so much better than being in my vehicle all day. I didn't stay there often. But that night when I tried to sleep in the basement and kept hearing the floors creak, that was the last time for me. Years later when I drove back to check on it, I saw that it was up for sale. I did my own personal walk through the house when they had an open house tour for the public and saw that they had changed everything. New hardwood floors, top of the line kitchen appliances, upgraded windows, it looked really nice. The furniture that was down there was gone, of course, but I wonder if my mom's spirit still visits at night. Someday, I will buy that place back. That house belongs to the McAdoo's. My grandparents, that I never met, lived in that house. Ever since then it has been passed down to their children. Ana Mae, my mother, grew up in that house. I did too. I view it as a collectable timepiece that a billionaire couldn't even get their hands on.

As a child, I had the mindset of whenever I came across tons of money, Mom could have whatever she wanted with the point of her finger. She deserved to live a life of luxury raising four kids by herself, but that day never came before her passing. Years later, I was informed when my biological dad had died. I felt nothing. There was a mental battle I was facing about whether to show up at the funeral or not. There was no need to pretend like I cared when he was never in my life. If I had attended, it would've made me feel like I was there only for attention. Nobody on his side of the family really knew me, because we didn't have that father and son bond.

Think about yourself. What are the things you would do on your bucket list if you only had $250 to your name, and only a month to live? Most people would travel to a specific destination. That was what I did. It was my dream to attend the University of Michigan then and go on to live an extravagant life that the NBA provided after being drafted. My dreams were cut short, but I felt the need to at least go there and experience what the atmosphere was like. I got mom's pills and headed out, thinking it would be the last place I ever traveled to. Everything seemed fine on the outside, but on the inside it was not. My mental health was total darkness. The things that went through my mind shouldn't be in anyone's, but it was normal to me. To disappear off the face of the earth seemed peaceful to me. That was one of many things that I look back on now and see how my mind was clouded and couldn't tell the difference between good and bad ideas. Even the bad ideas seemed good at times. And mom's pills were going to help end the story of my life when my situation got too extreme for me to handle.

When I pulled up to the University, it was like a now or never moment. I was filled with curiosity. Standing outside the buildings taking pictures with my disposable camera wasn't enough. I needed to go in and get the authentic experience. When you have nothing to lose, that's when you find out the real you and stop letting your fears control your present and future. A quote I read that stuck with me is,

"The person that overcomes their fears will *truly* be free."

I thought, what is the worst that could happen? Me getting kicked off campus. Even if one of the scenarios *possibly* led me to being put behind bars, I was still going to give myself an exclusive tour. I had come too far to turn back. I took pictures of the classrooms, game room, library, anything that I saw as interesting. It was a disposable camera, so I had to take pictures that I knew were special and not waste film.

With very little money coming in, I needed to find a better way of selling Mom's pills. A lot of people didn't know about it, because I wasn't in the drug game for attention. It was for survival purposes only. I could have easily had the mindset of getting one of my homies on the block to grant me the knowledge of becoming a drug dealer, but that would only have made matters worse and left me feeling more paranoid than I already was. I am thankful for my strong mindset when it came to that, but it was weak in other areas.

If it wasn't for me putting my pride aside and going to the biohazard center to donate blood plasma, I don't know what I would have done. I maybe only told a couple people at Labor Forcer about the pills and made sure they didn't tell anyone else. All our pockets were turned inside out, that's why we were all there, to get extra work, to keep income flowing in some kind of way. A few guys that worked for Labor Forcer were doing some bad things that I didn't want to be involved in. If they got caught and kicked off the job, they had family to go back to. But me? Nope. I would be digging myself a grave.

As you have read the story, you probably realized that the pills were always within my reach. I didn't have to call around for them or put out the word that I needed some, so why wouldn't I profit from them? The time where the police officer saw the pills in my possession, words couldn't explain how I felt. If I got anything out of that situation it was that not all cops are bad. He could have easily made up a story of me selling them and taken me to jail, and that would have been the end of everything. No family to call from jail. No money for me to get commissary. No vehicle to go back to when I got out. Nothing! I would have gone from living the luxury life of the homeless, to sleeping under a bridge or staying in a tent. How would I have picked myself back up? I guess we will never find out, thank God!

So, I was doing good for a while, not back tracking by messing with Ladonna. Then the good old times started to play out in my head. That led us to become not a couple exactly, but friends with benefits. The make-up sex was too good to forget. She and I knew that was both of our weaknesses, even though we were wanting to let each other go. I would have, if Tracy would've given me a chance, but what can you do? When it came time to call up people to attend my graduation ceremony, both of them came to mind. But somehow I knew what their answers would have been, which would've been a confident no. Inviting my family was a hard decision. If they would have given me the same answer, that would've torn my heart apart. From the fear of them declining my invite, I decided to play it safe and celebrate my success alone. Even though it hurt without them being there, it didn't break me.

Was it worth being in debt $15,000 after graduating college? Yes. I watched the Chris Hogan podcast: *Don't be a victim to your credit score*, and he read an article, that came from another source, that discussed why nearly half of indebted millennials say college wasn't worth the investment. Some students that are no longer in debt say college was worth it. When I went to tech college, I knew that being an electrician was a smart choice. It's a field that you can never stop learning in, since there is innovative technology created every year.

While attending trade school, my teacher told the class that we could skip college and graduate debt free by applying for an electrical company that would pay our way through apprenticeship school, but only if you kept your grades up during the process. If you didn't, then you would have to pay back all the money the company had put in. The courses that I took transferred over. Therefore, I was skipped ahead when it came time for me to transition to apprentice school after trying to prove that I wasn't in my right year. It was my desire to attend a university first, but I highly appreciated the tech school education. It still was a form of higher education that will better my life overall. It would be a waste of time to spend that amount of money on a career that didn't need a degree to flourish in. Even if I had gone to a university to get a master's degree, my salary would have still been the same starting out! There was no company that would hire me without experience, so I used a tech college education as a tool to get me in the door to show them how serious I was about my career. In the interview for my first job, at Great Links Electric, the interviewer was on the fence about hiring me.

"We only hire people with experience, even to be a helper, but how are you supposed to get experience when no one will hire you?" he said.

Then I spoke about me attending school, and showed him my college portfolio of all the things I was learning in school. That is what secured the deal. Even though I still have over $12,000 from student loans to pay back at the time of this writing, but it was worth the investment to attend college.

I was a late bloomer at starting to make payments after I graduated. The fear of paying it, then a crisis happen where I couldn't keep the consistency of making payments up is why I didn't work on erasing my debt right out of school. The interest would put the balance back up to where it once was, and all the money I would've spent paying it down would have been pointless. Little did

I know, the interest on my loans was great! Less than five percent. I figured all this out years later, and now tackling the debt with full vengeance.

My times of getting kicked out of different spots while homeless were stressful. This is what life is all about - adjusting to unexpected changes. It seemed hard at first, but once I knew there were many spots to choose from, that was when things started to look up for me… until it got old. Struggling alone with no home and taking bird baths at different stores like that would put a strain on anyone. I had tried the best I could to hold on, but life was kicking my ass and it eventually came time for me to tap out. It felt as if my life had reached its end. There was a time when I tried to borrow a pistol from someone I knew. This was after my coke experience, so my mind was numb to any and everything except for sex. It was good that he didn't give it to me. If I wasn't going to use it on someone, then I would've used it on myself. That would be a sure way of ending it all with the squeeze of a trigger instead of swallowing pills trying to overdose. I thought that would surely take me out as well, but God was clearly not finished with me yet. There are still hearts I must touch through the words of my books. It share's most of my dark times to inspire others to overcome obstacles that seem impossible to bare. I feel that's the reason I've been put through so much.

That time I took the whole bottle of sleeping pills and sliced open my wrist was a scary one. I was depressed and didn't know it. Depression is deadly like that. It can sneak up on you before you even realize it. Once you do, it could be too late. Luckily for me, God had a better ending for me than to leave this earth like that. I thank Ladonna for letting me know what depression felt like, because I had no clue. I had always heard that word, but never researched it to know what it feels like and how to overcome it, or the signs that it's trying to work its way in. The number of pills that I took and snorted at the motel would've caused most people to overdose, even on less than half the amount. God was telling me there was a bigger purpose for my life, and the same is true for others who tried to commit suicide and failed. Without a test there's no testimony. We all have a destiny to fulfill, and suicide is not in those plans.

There are some things in this book that I didn't want to express to the world, but it would mean that everything I went through was pointless. What makes this a unique story is the tragic events and scary attempts that were made, and I don't regret any of it. It helped mold me into the person I have become. Today I am stronger, wiser, and better equipped because of it and can offer some of the tools to help other people get over their depression. Holding everything will only damage yourself. After going to C.S.U, I thought they would be the ones to make me feel better, but I was wrong. I was truthful when I gave my story about the reason I was in there, but it still didn't help. A female best friend was all I wanted. Someone that was trustworthy and could keep secrets. Someone that was beautiful, inside and out. Someone that wouldn't judge my circumstance. She was nowhere to be found, so I kept quiet. It's hard for some people to reveal their flaws in front of a group full of strangers. There was a quote that I thought was interesting,

"If you ever want to tell a secret, put it in a book."

Not everyone reads books, but the people that are meant to receive the message will get it or hear about it. "God gives His toughest battles to His strongest warriors," is another powerful quote I like to remember. It boils down to what you do with the situation after the battle is won. Some keep it all in and pretend like they're perfect, but I want to be brave and to shed light on someone that might be going through the same challenging times. Some people aren't brave enough to express themselves because of what other people may think. Sometimes I get like that, but then I realize people made fun of Jesus, who was perfect, so what makes you think people won't bash you? You can be the best looking, or have the most money, but there will always be something people can or will criticize you for.

When my SUV broke down and the mechanic looked at it, the price was through the roof to fix it. I gave the car dealership a call to pick it up at the motel that I was living in. I told them the keys would be in the car, with the doors unlocked. That stopped all the incoming calls at night. It was wrong for me to keep riding in it without making payments, but that was my only means of survival. After that, they took me to court and sued me for the rest of the money that was owed. Me and the lawyer talked about how much I could pay every month until it was paid off. “As long as you are making some kind of reasonable payment every month it is okay.”

I started off doing great then, after about six months, I started to slip. I thought there was at least $10,000 that I still owed, but when I checked it was around $5,000 and that gave me a boost of energy to get it knocked out. That sounds a lot better than $10,000, so the only thing for me to do was pay it off to get them out of my way. That was my second time being sued, and it did not feel good. Now that is over, I can move on with my life.

Eating alone during Thanksgiving was depressing. My plan was to get some tasty food and chill out by myself at the table. Like I said, I figured I already was alone and so what difference would it make? Turns out there was a significant difference when surrounded by other people, with their tables full of fun and mine full of sadness. That’s why I told myself on Christmas, I wouldn’t be alone. That was before I ever knew that I was going to be living with Samantha in the country. Especially on those two holidays, nobody should ever be alone. It was a mistake trying to experience it by myself. A mistake that I wouldn’t make again. On Christmas, Samantha’s family, Tre-Tre, and I had a blast. My son didn’t care that he had to spend it separately from his parents. All he could understand was that he was getting presents from me and then more at his mom’s. If he is happy, then that’s all that matters.

I didn’t feel guilty about not taking him on the trip to Florida. There was a lot that I had been through and needed to let loose. It would be hard for me to do that with him there, and also there was a fear that he wouldn’t like to get on the plane. The day eventually came when I tested him to see if he was scared to fly. For his first flight, we went to Venice Beach in California. He didn’t care about the high altitude, his focus was on the monitor watching a movie during our whole flight!

Samantha and I were one solid pair that almost nothing could break apart. When it came down to her and the kids, it got too overwhelming for me. How do I manage taking care of kids when I was barely taking care of myself? I believe we could have been a lifelong couple. She was always curious about how our relationship was going to turn out. At first, meeting them seemed okay, but as time went on, they needed her increasingly more. I saw it would be hard for us to keep our relationship exciting, as we both were spontaneous.

One Sunday after church, I asked if she wanted to go to Gatlinburg, TN with me. Just a quick pop-up trip. I'd never been, but had always heard wonderful stories about the town.

"Are you forreal?!"

"Yeah! It's only a couple hours away. We can go down there and come back the same day, since I have work tomorrow."

She kept on trying to call my bluff, but I was serious. I drove home so she could change clothes. My intentions were to go right then and there! We hadn't even left the church parking lot when I came up with the idea and wanted to head straight there. When we got there, we barely could see anything. Nightfall came quicker than I'd expected it to.

"Let's stay the night and get a room," she said.

I was willing to do it since it would be a waste of time to go all the way down there to see nothing and then drive right back home. When the next day came, we went out on the strip and had tons of fun not doing much but sightseeing. That's what I liked about her. When something fun comes to mind I want to do it right then if I can, and whenever there was time, she would be right there beside me and ready for an unexpected adventure. What I loved about Brittany and her is they are very generous when helping others, even if they didn't know them. Like the old saying goes, "All good things must come to an end." Our relationship did just that. Overall, I wasn't ready to take on the responsibilities of helping to raise her kids, so we ended it on a good note. She found a partner, who later became her fiancé to fill that gap. I hope he can keep her happy the way I did. Those are big shoes to fill. I am still not married. If God can match me up with Samantha, and the only thing that was wrong was the kids and age gap, which was over 6 years, then I know there is a woman out there with the same beautiful soul and less kids that would love to live a life of surprises by my side. Granny was over 60 years old when she passed. Being 100% Black and having a white granny may seem weird to most, but if we were ever seen in public together, I would just say, “this is my albino grandma,” to lessen the confusion and questions.

Years have flown by since the last time I saw my family. I thought that was the end of our family relationship. They were focused on them, and I was focused on me. Even when I was writing my first book: *Lost in My World*, I had no intention of telling them. I knew they would find out eventually from me marketing my book on different social media outlets. With the fear of being rejected again, it was best to stay clear of potential disappointment. When I put the first letter down for my debut book, there was no turning back. And with that being the first book I wrote, after doing hours of research on how to write a book, it turned out to be great for my first-time writing. My plan is to get better with the books I produce in the future, and then hopefully, one day they will transition to the big screen.

On Father’s Day, I wanted to visit my previous church that most of my family members attended. Nobody outside of my immediate family knew about our issue. I haven’t been there in a long time, and wanted to show my son where I first started going to church. I saw my sister sitting downstairs. She waved and wanted to meet up after church. I haven’t seen her in *years*! We went out to eat and spoke about the past. We both wished the situation never ended the way that it did. But that is all behind us now. It was a temporary circumstance that became a part of my testimony to tell. Four years later, after finally rising above the fear of getting close to them and then becoming an outsider again, that situation was over. On Christmas of 2019, all of us got together and became a family again. We took a group photo. It was my first time seeing them again, and it wasn’t as awkward as I thought it would be. We picked right back up where we had left off. The last time I’d shared a holiday with anyone in my family was back in 2010. It hasn’t seemed that long ago until I looked at the year gap. With the help of my strong support system that I’ve accumulated over the years, I feel it would be near impossible for me to relive the past. In October of 2020 I moved out of Brittany’s house and got my own *luxury* apartment that I always fantasized about while I was homeless. Just me and my son living under one roof, comfortably. This was not the end, but the beginning of my story. Welcome.